Tall Betsy and Dunce Baby

South Georgia Folktales

Tall Betsy and Dunce Baby

South Georgia Folktales

Mariella Glenn Hartsfield

The University of Georgia Press

Athens and London

© 1987 by the University of Georgia Press
Athens, Georgia 30602
All rights reserved

Designed by Kathi L. Dailey
Set in Mergenthaler Goudy Old Style
Typeset by The Composing Room of Michigan
Printed and bound by Braun-Brumfield
The paper in this book meets the guidelines for
permanence and durability of the Committee on
Production Guidelines for Book Longevity of the Council
on Library Resources.

Printed in the United States of America

91 90 89 88 87   5 4 3 2 1

Library of Congress Cataloging in Publication Data

Hartsfield, Mariella Glenn.
Tall Betsy and Dunce Baby.

Bibliography: p.
Includes index.
1. Tales—Georgia. 2. Georgia—Social life and customs.
3. Tall tales—Georgia. 4. Storytellers—Georgia. I. Title.
GR110.G4H37   1987   398.2'09758   86-11360
ISBN 0-8203-0900-1

British Library Cataloging in Publication Data available.

There are times so beautiful
that touch our lives so deeply
the passing takes with it life
and the want of another season

In appreciation and love to
my mother and father

Marie Cupper Glenn
William Robert Glenn

Contents

Contents

Contents

Acknowledgments

My appreciation goes first and foremost to the people of southwest Georgia, especially those in the rural areas who worked and loved the land. To these and to the great storytellers who have flourished here I owe a debt of gratitude, for this book is their story.

I am also much indebted to the following professors at Florida State University who supported and encouraged my interest in the field of folklore: Fred Standley, Francis Townsend, Hardin Goodman, John Priest, and Russell Reaver. It was in Professor Reaver's folklore class that my field work in folklore began. After that course, I undertook additional studies at the University of Utah with Professor Jan Harold Brunvand. These two folklorists introduced me to a discipline that spans all times and cultures. My awareness of the continuity of life and of the human spirit will be forever expanded by this introduction.

Constant support and encouragement have also come from family and friends: Glenn and Susan Pelham (who served as readers for the manuscript), Ellie Glenn, Mary Frances and Clarke Maxwell, Naomi and Bill Oliver, Harriette and Bob Hamrick, Anne Marie Oliver, Lew Oliver, Eva Maxwell, Reynolds Maxwell, Dale McColskey, Nancy Goodyear, Deborah Miller Sommer, Virginia Wilson, Sarah Paulk, Richard Hoops, Joyce Nelson, Susan Ellzey, Cindy King Taylor, and Yvonne Brunton.

There are still others to whom I am most appreciative: to Wessie Connell, director of the nationally acclaimed Roddenbery Memorial Library in Cairo, and Barbara Williams, associate director, for their commitment to preserving invaluable county history; to the *Cairo Messenger* and its editors for their assistance in research; to the Grady County English teachers for their contributions and suggestions; to former student Nancy Long, who assisted in the transcription and typing of numerous tapes; to

Acknowledgments

Delta Kappa Gamma Society for granting me an International Scholarship to pursue my studies in folklore; to President Ed Mobley and Dean Fred Henderson of Bainbridge Junior College for granting release time to complete this project; and especially to John A. Hartsfield, Jr. (Johnny), who believed in this study so much that he accompanied me during all the taping sessions and served as the photographer and recorder. To him I am indebted most of all, for without his constant encouragement and assistance this book would not have become a reality.

Preface

The person who wishes to discover truths about the folktale, more formally called the traditional prose narrative, must approach the study with the tenacity of a Menelaus wrestling with Proteus. Stoutheartedly, he grasps the prose narrative only to find that, Proteus-like, it constantly changes and evolves, exhibiting different faces and moods with differing times and milieus. Yet the fascination of studying the changes and variations is not unlike that of watching clouds drift, change forms, and combine with other clouds. John Ruskin used such imagery in describing the folk "story" in his introduction to Grimm's *German Popular Stories:* "The story remains essentially true, altering its form, indeed like a flying cloud, but remaining a sign of the sky; a shadowy image, as truly a part of the great firmament of the human mind as the light of reason which it seems to interrupt."[1] Folktales, like man who keeps them alive, defy finality. They may experience addition, deletion, or synthesis but never rigidity as long as they have life.

My interest in folktales was not always so analytical; certainly any appreciation of their stability amid constantly changing forms totally eluded me. In short, all that I can say about my experience with folktales in earlier years is that I was inundated with them. But as we are indifferent to so many valuable and memorable experiences surrounding us in childhood because of their proximity to us, so are we unappreciative of folktales except in retrospect. So it was in my own childhood; I took these tales for granted, assuming that all children knew such stories. For generations storytelling had been in my family on the paternal

1. John Ruskin, introduction to *German Popular Stories,* ed. Edgar Taylor (London: Chatto & Windus, 1892), p. x.

1

side, and the role of storyteller seemed to settle on my father. Whether it was before the fire on winter nights, at meals, at the tobacco barn, at cane grindings, or anywhere the family might gather, my father would begin to lure us into his tales with such a line as "That reminds me of the time . . . ." His repertoire of stories included ghost tales, Pat and Mike (the two Irishmen) stories, church anecdotes, stories of courtship, and hundreds of reminiscences. From the time that my three sisters and I could talk, walk, and remember, we were always asking that these stories be told over and over again.

We were especially enchanted with visits from two ghosts (albeit benevolent ones) who lived in the attic over the kitchen— Tall Betsy and her little child, Dunce Baby. Both of these revenants appeared many times to us through the years, so much so that we thought it was fairly natural and probably universally true that all children knew of these creatures. When the family occasionally moved to a new location in the county, Tall Betsy and Dunce Baby apparently packed their bags as well and moved with us. Some verities are never questioned, much less explained, and the relocation of Tall Betsy and her offspring in our household was among such verities.

On a cold winter night we might see a flash of Tall Betsy, a looming creature with flowing white robes, outside the bedroom window. Or we might be permitted to come slowly into a dimly lit bedroom and meet Dunce Baby, complete with cap and long dress, beside the bed. These were part of our tradition, perpetuated from one generation to the next. In years to come I found myself creating and holding high a Tall Betsy (a sheet-draped broom suspended over my head) on a cold winter night and running wildly past a window through which my little nieces and nephews peered with large saucer eyes. If the children were really good, I would approach the ghosts' attic home, call up at the opening, and politely ask Tall Betsy if Dunce Baby could visit us for a while. Thus, on many a Sunday afternoon or during a holiday, I found myself lying under the bed, flat on my stomach, with elbows on the floor just out from the cover and hands covered with dress, cap, and a little painted face. When the questions

2

came from the children as to the preferences of Dunce Baby (all of which were as traditional as the answers), I would nod or shake Dunce Baby's head (formed by clasping my hands together) and become the shadowy instructional figure generations old.

And the questions poured forth for the mute little ghost: "Do you like chocolate Hershey bars, Dunce Baby? Do you like turnips? Do you like liver? Do you like castor oil? Will you do a little dance for us?" Interestingly enough, but appropriate to his instructional use, Dunce Baby did not like Hershey bars but loved turnips, collards, and liver. Although he did not mind taking castor oil, he drew the line at nodding yes to the question "Dunce Baby, do you mind getting spankings if you've been bad?" He would simply hang his head to one side and turn his little body as if shrugging off this painful question.

These shadowy but humorous creatures were a part of our lives along with others who were unseen and intangible (and hence more frightening), such as Mr. Rawhide and Bloody Bones, and the ominous Black Dog (at least ten feet high). The mere mention of these two apparitions lurking outside the house would end any argument between sisters and ensure that directives from our mother would be acted upon ere they were given.

Thus our lives were filled with numerous fictional characters and many, many stories. It took a course at Florida State University under Professor Russell Reaver, however, to make me realize not only that these tales were worthy of scholarly study but that they could also yield much significant information about the heritage of the area in which they circulated. So began a collection of tales from Grady County in southwest Georgia and a scholarly interest in the world of the folktale. This interest later resulted in one year of intensive study of folklore at the University of Utah with Professor Jan Harold Brunvand, author of the very popular classroom textbook *The Study of American Folkore.*

Much to my chagrin, I soon learned that the fledging folklorist, unlike a veteran collector such as Richard Dorson, usually has difficulties both in locating excellent storytellers and in asking the right questions to elicit the tales. To collect a mass of folktales while attending a wedding in Milwaukee may seem all in a day's work for the Richard Dorsons of this world. But I found it a hard task to uncover the treasures even in my own backyard.

To identify the storytellers within the community, I mapped out the following strategy: write a series of articles for the local paper, the *Cairo Messenger,* meet with the Grady County Council of the Teachers of English, and go into the high schools with a discussion of the folktale.

The *Cairo Messenger* was most cooperative in my journalistic endeavors to secure some Grady County folktales and even featured several articles on the folktale. In one article, "The Folktale: A Mirror of the Grady County People," I included names of some of my early contacts, hoping that by citing individuals and their contributions, other contacts would follow. A second article followed giving an example of two Grady County tales, a tall tale by Mr. Allen Womble and a humorous anecdote by Mr. Robert Glenn. Both articles stimulated much interest and discussion and produced a few informants. One of these was Mr. M. P. Maxwell, a delightful source of tall tales and a reservoir of local history who contacted me by mail offering to write his stories instead of recording them on tape. Later, however, Mr. Maxwell did agree to being interviewed but would tell only those stories he thought appropriate for a lady. In spite of my protests to forget my gender, Mr. Maxwell's Southern, gentlemanly breeding prevailed in the end; he did, however, concede to include some of these ribald stories in a letter.

Next I met with the local English teachers under the direction of Eleanor Griffies, chairman of the English department at Cairo High School. I whipped out all my prepared packets for each teacher, discussed at length what type of folklore I was soliciting, played a recording of a humorous tale, and asked their assistance in the project.

Wessie Connell, head librarian and the prime mover behind the nationally acclaimed Roddenbery Memorial Library in Cairo, was most supportive and urged students and teachers to submit names of storytellers to the library for me. Then I sat back, fully expecting to be deluged with names of great storytellers. Much to my disappointment, only a few dribbled in. The teachers, although quite enthusiastic over the collection of oral tales, felt that I would achieve quicker and better results if I implemented my next plan of action—visit the classrooms and talk with students in person.

My discussions in the classrooms did prove to be my most fruitful move. When the students heard the actual recording of a ghost tale told by an outstanding narrator, such as Mr. Robert Glenn, they enthusiastically thronged about me at the end of class, suggesting parents, grandfathers, or aunts and uncles who had told them stories in the past. Once the momentum picked up, I was asked to speak before other groups: a tri-county bookclub, a tri-county honorary teachers' organization, Bainbridge Junior College Forum, and the Decatur County Historical Society—all of which supplied additional names.

In the actual collecting I developed a new respect for the veteran field-workers, such as Elsie Clews Parsons, who have devoted so much time to the preservation of folk traditions, especially in the prerecorder days. I was fortunate to have a companion accompany me in all the taping sessions—John A. Hartsfield, Jr. (Johnny), who captured in photographs the informants in various poses during the storytelling process. Prior to each session, we would note either in writing or on the recorder the name of the informant, the date of the taping, the makeup of the audience, and any other pertinent information about the event. We soon learned some important rules to follow in taping the sessions: do not frighten the informant by shoving the microphone too quickly in his face (in fact, after one discouraging interview, we traded in our old recorder for a newer model with a built-in microphone); try to sit as close to the informant as possible with the recorder unobtrusively nearby; do not place the recorder by a fan or an air conditioner; and do not even discuss the recorder until the situation is at ease and the narrator relaxed. In fact, we found that the less said about the equipment, the more at ease the informant was. At the end of these sessions we would usually replay part of the tape for the informant, especially if he had never heard himself on tape.

Many times informants would protest that they knew nothing that would be worthy of recording. Indeed it was difficult to distinguish for them what we were actually seeking. Comments would vary: "All I know is some true stories"; "You wouldn't want to record the stories I know"; or "I know some funny stories told about people around here. Do you want that?" Johnny and I changed our approach considerably in later interviews: instead of trying to lead the informant too quickly in the beginning, we allowed ourselves to be led by him. For many informants a folktale or two might be imbedded within several hours of local history. And frequently, hours of local history would yield just that—only local history. Yet much of this material proved invaluable in establishing the context for the tales. If the informant was a natural raconteur (and such is rare), then stories flowed forth rather quickly; with others, procurement of some tale might necessitate a return visit. We did make a point of returning to one storyteller to record the same story with a different audience.

We discovered that the acceptance of any offers of food (such as cake, homemade soup, boiled peanuts) or even cuttings of flowers helped to establish rapport quickly. Even to move from a living room to a more informal setting, such as the kitchen or side porch, would break the ice and cause conversation to flow more easily. One of our best interviews was conducted while sitting on the grass next to a barn. But when there is much moving around, the collector must make absolutely certain that recorder batteries are in good working order.

In the final analysis, the collector of folklore must have endless patience, perseverance, and a willingness to give himself over to the situation. The more he can become a part of the informant's world, the more likely he is to record some excellent material.

Types of Folktales Found in Southwest Georgia

Several questions emerged while soliciting names of narrators and even while interviewing narrators. "What do you mean when you say *folktale?* Just what is a folktale? How does it differ from, say, the myth or the legend?" And it is true that many terms (myth, legend, folktale, etc.) are bandied about when considering the prose narrative, for lines of demarcation remain tenuous at best.

Some scholars, such as Stith Thompson, seem to shun the need for exact terminology yet proceed to make at least some minimal but helpful distinctions. In 1946, with the publication of *The Folktale,* Thompson maintained, "Much hair-splitting has taken place in the past and much useless effort devoted to the establishment of exact terms for various kinds of folktales. Yet some very general terms are not only very helpful but necessary."[2]

In 1955, in an addendum to a symposium on the folktale, he was still asking, "But why should myth be accurately defined? Is there actually any need to differentiate, for example, between such concepts as mythology and hero tales?"[3] He did finally conclude, however, that there was practical value in defining myths according to their subject matter but not according to origin.

In an important article in 1965, anthropologist William Bascom sought to bring some agreement among professional scholars from both the humanities and the social sciences by directing his discussion toward a definition of myth, legend, and folktale. Jan Brunvand, in citing Bascom's article in his chapter on myths and legends, summarizes Bascom's approach quite succinctly: "Myths are distinguished from legends by the attitudes of the storytellers toward them, the settings described in them, and their principal characters."[4] Bascom cautioned the reader, however, against assuming that the myth, legend, and folktale are "necessarily the only major categories of prose narratives, under which all other kinds of prose narratives must be classified as sub-types."[5] They are, nevertheless, three of the most frequently discussed and debated types of the prose narrative, and distinctions among them

2. Stith Thompson, *The Folktale* (New York: Dryden Press, 1946), p. 7.

3. Stith Thompson, "Myths and Folktales," JAF 68 (1955): 484.

4. Jan Harold Brunvand, *The Study of American Folklore* (New York: W. W. Norton and Co., 1968), p. 79.

5. William Bascom, "The Forms of Folklore: Prose Narratives," JAF 78 (1965): 5.

are most pertinent for a functional-anthropological approach to folklore.

Table 1 utilizes Bascom's distinctions among the three types of prose narratives but incorporates Brunvand's summary of the anthropologist's approach. The three types are not always clearly separated, as the lines of demarcation are tenuous. Bascom repeatedly reminded his readers: "It is entirely possible that the same tale type may be a folktale in one society, a legend in a second society, and a myth in a third. . . . It is also worth knowing that certain narratives were formerly believed as myth or legend, and which tales are losing (or gaining) credence" (p. 9). In her essay "Folk Narrative," Hungarian folkorist Linda Dégh corroborates such fluctuation among narrative types. "The genres are always variable. Identical stories can be found within different genres. What is a tale for one culture may be an origin legend for another; a twist in a tragic story for one can render it extremely funny for another."[6]

In *The Folktale* Stith Thompson states that among the classes of prose narratives, myth is the most confusing to distinguish. One characteristic, however, upon which most folklorists seem to concur is that the myth is connected with "religious beliefs and practices of the people" (p. 9). Even with this commonly accepted criterion of myth, Maria Leach's *Standard Dictionary of Folklore, Mythology, and Legend* adds the following qualification: "A myth remains properly a myth only as long as the divinity of its act or actors is recognized; when the trickster becomes human rather than divine, when the hero is a man rather than a god, myth becomes legend, if explanatory or limited to one specific location; or folktale, if more generalized."[7] The setting of the myth is of another place and time, removed from the present-day environment.

The legend, like the myth, is also considered a fact, although

6. Linda Dégh, "Folk Narrative," in *Folklore and Folklife: An Introduction*, ed. Richard M. Dorson (Chicago: University of Chicago Press, 1973), p. 59.

7. Maria Leach, ed., *Standard Dictionary of Folklore, Mythology, and Legend* (New York: Funk and Wagnalls Co., 1949), 2:778.

Table 1. Three Types of Prose Narrative

	Legend (Sagen, traditions populaire)	Myth (Mythen, mythes)	Folktale (*Märchen,* contes populaire)
Attitude of storyteller toward narrative	Sacred or secular, fact	Sacred, fact	Secular, fiction
Setting	Recent past, world of today	Remote past, different world	Anytime, anyplace
Characters	Human	Nonhuman	Human or nonhuman

as Richard Dorson suggests, "The word *legend* implies an exaggerated and colorful account of an event." However, Dorson continues, "Because they purport to be historical and factual, they must be associated in the mind of the community with some known individual, geographical landmark, or particular episode. . . . This is indeed one of the main tests of a legend, that it be known to a number of people united by their area of residence or occupation or nationality or faith."[8] In short, the legend is a prose narrative purporting to be based upon some historical happening, location, or person and set in the recent past or world of today, using humans as principal characters and possessing a recognizable structure.

In juxtaposing the legend with the folktale (*Märchen*), both William Bascom in his article on the prose narrative and Linda Dégh in her chapter on the folk narrative seek to delineate the distinctions between the two types by citing Jacob Grimm in his preface to the second edition of *Deutsche Mythologie* (1844).

8. Richard M. Dorson, "Legends and Tall Tales," in *Our Living Traditions: An Introduction to American Folklore,* ed. Tristram Potter Coffin (New York: Basic Books, 1968), pp. 154–55.

Dégh maintains that after more than 120 years scholars have added very little to the following concise statement made by Grimm: "The fairy-tale [*Märchen*] is with good reason distinguished from the Legend, though by turns they play into one another. Looser, less fettered than legend, the fairy-tale lacks that local habitation, which hampers the legend, but makes it more homelike. The fairy-tale flies, the legend walks, knocks at your door; the one can draw freely out of the fullness of poetry, the other has almost the authority of history" (p. 72). Grimm's use of the verb *flies* perhaps capsules the essence of the folktale; it is of the imagination, not bound to any time or place. It is secular and fiction and comprised of either human or nonhuman characters.

Of these three types of prose narratives it is the folktale that is most dominant in Grady County. A few legends are included in the collection, but the main interest lies with the fictional prose narrative. Even with this narrowing there are still complexities, for the subtypes of folktales are numerous and varied, ranging from the very complex *Märchen* to the simpler jest or humorous anecdote.

There are many possibilities for cataloging the different forms of folktales. One of the most common divisions is that used by Stith Thompson in his *Type Index* in which he designates the following four types: (1) animal tales, (2) ordinary folktales, (3) jokes and anecdotes, and (4) formula tales. His second division, ordinary folktales, seems too all-inclusive, however, to identify clearly the forms of folktales extant in Grady County. Thompson in *The Folktale*, however, makes very definite distinctions between the complex tale and the simple tale, defining the latter as having usually a single narrative motif, whereas the more complex tale might contain numerous motifs and have episodic sequences. In her chapter on the folk narrative Dégh, in establishing also her tale genres by use of simple-complex designations, lists subdivisions under each that have been utilized in figure 1.

Under complex tales she enumerates three of Thompson's types: (1) the *Märchen* or magic tale, (2) the religious tale, and (3) the novella or romantic tale (pp. 62–68). The *Märchen* is a term widely used with no clear equivalent in English. Frequently,

Figure 1. The Folktale

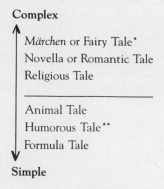

Complex

Märchen or Fairy Tale*
Novella or Romantic Tale
Religious Tale

Animal Tale
Humorous Tale**
Formula Tale

Simple

*A few found in Grady County.
**Predominant type found in Grady County.

it is used interchangeably with the term *folktale* and serves as a general category under which many forms of prose narratives are covered. In this study it is used merely as one form of the folktale—that form which has the most complex structure of all the folktales and is synonymous with the fairy tale. Thompson, although using it in its broadest sense, defines it as "a tale of some length involving a succession of motifs or episodes. It moves in an unreal world without definite locality or definite characters and is filled with the marvelous. In this never-never land humble heroes kill adversaries, succeed to kingdoms and marry princesses" (*The Folktale*, p. 8). Some of the Grady County tales fall into this category, although with some qualification. Most folklorists agree that the real *Märchen* as previously defined is seldom found in modern times, especially in America. The tales in southwest Georgia so categorized are those of a supernatural nature and somewhat longer and more complex than the single motif narrative but are certainly not of the complexity of such fairy tales as "Cinderella," "Snow White," or "Hansel and Gretel."

No religious tale appears in this collection and only one novella. The former, as defined by Dégh, "deals with Christian virtues and has a close relationship with Christian legend. Its personnel are divided between vicious and virtuous human beings and supernatural characters" (p. 66). The novella, unlike the *Märchen*, tends toward a more realistic world of a definite time and place. The sources of many of these romantic tales are frequently literary.

Most of the Grady County tales fall into simpler structural classifications, primarily that of "humorous tales." This category deviates from Dégh's (Thompson's) classification of "jokes and anecdotes." Again, as Jan Brunvand points out, Thompson's category is troublesome, for both jokes and anecdotes are misleading in that jokes imply primarily modern traditions and anecdotes call to mind the personal legend. Both are imprecise terms for the fictional prose narratives found in Georgia. They are more closely related to the German work *Schwank*, which Dégh calls "the most elaborate of the humorous narrative . . . a relatively long, well-structured, realistic narrative without fantastic or miraculous motifs" (p. 70). These tales may deal with foolish persons who act absurdly, unsaintly persons, and deceiving spouses or suitors. The tellers of the *Schwank*, unlike tellers of jokes, have a very stable repertoire of material and usually perform for audiences.

The animal tale, as classified in the strictest sense, has not been recorded in Grady County, even though one or two tales do have animals that occasionally carry out some human function. In this division animals are the principal characters and assume the role of humans. Although this type is used sometimes synonymously with the fable, the fable is also frequently considered a subtype of the animal tale. For Thompson it is the moral purpose which "distinguishes the fable from the other animal tales" (p. 10).

Formula tales, Dégh's last division under simple tales, represent a very old category of folktales, according to Brunvand (p. 117). These tales have a very strict, structural pattern usually involving repetition and built more around stylistic devices than content, such as "House that Jack Built." None of these has been found in the Grady County area, however.

At best, categories are a tentative and sometimes an ephemeral means of clarification in most disciplines and are especially so in folklore. If some illumination comes from having set up temporary boundaries for this study, then perhaps they are justified and even welcomed.

In his foreword to *Bloodstoppers and Bearwalkers*, Richard Dorson reached this optimistic conclusion: "No field collector can of course investigate all of the United States, or even a succession of regions, in one lifetime. But fieldwork done in depth in a relatively limited area can illuminate the entire American scene."[9] My aim in this collection was a modest one—namely, to collect folktales in my own home county of Grady and to analyze the findings. The results of this study, although somewhat less than an illumination of the entire American scene perhaps, certainly bring to light a heritage reaching far from its provincial beginning.

After choosing one county for my exploration, I narrowed my focus even more by choosing only white storytellers who have been longtime residents in the county and whose heritage dates back at least one generation. The decision to include only white narrators was made for one primary reason: I planned to follow this collection of tales with its appropriate sequel—a collection of black tales. I felt that by studying the tales separately, I could analyze the individual canons more thoroughly. There is also in the collection a noticeable absence of ribald or obscene folktales, many of which do exist in the county. The problem lay in my gender; the Southern narrators refused to tell these to a "lady," and even when they did write them down, they made me promise that I would not include them in the collection—all of which attests once again to the power of custom and tradition in the South. My purpose in this collection was to look thoroughly and holistically at the storytelling continuum—the function and setting of the tales, the character of the narrators, the forms of the tales, the narrative style of the outstanding storytellers, and even in a limited way the influence of the county newspaper on folktales.

The format for annotating the tales took a different turn from

9. Richard Dorson, *Bloodstoppers and Bearwalkers* (Cambridge: Harvard University Press, 1972), p. viii.

that of many collections. Beyond the assignment of types and motifs, which has become a fairly common but useful device among folklorists, I wanted to compare variants predominantly from North America and England to gain not only some notion of the heritage of the tales but to study, as well, the significant changes made in transmission from one locale to another and to note important structural modifications. Such a comparative study is by no means exhaustive, for I lay no claim to having accumulated every North American and English version of each tale.

The classification of Grady County tales according to types and motifs, as given at the end of this study (see Appendix 3), should provide assistance to folklore scholars, but, more important, it indicates the range of tales found in Grady County. Of the thirty-two subdivisions established by Aarne and Thompson in *The Types of the Folktale,* the Grady County collection makes contributions to nine of these: supernatural adversaries, novella (romantic tales), numskull stories, stories about married couples, stories about a woman (girl), the stupid man, jokes about parsons and religious orders, anecdotes about other groups of people, and tales of lying. In the classifications by motifs, fifty-four identifiable motifs were found in this study and ten new Georgia subdivisions established. The motifs fell under nine of Thompson's main divisions in *The Motif-Index:* the dead, ogres, tests, the wise and the foolish, deceptions, chance and fate, sex, traits of character, and humor. The large number of tales fell under "J. The Wise and the Foolish" and "X. Humor," although there was a substantial tradition of tales related to the dead and to witch lore. Most of the tales for which no variants could be found were in the humorous division, under jokes about ministers and tall tales. For many of these, new subdivisions were proposed (indicated by Georgia abbreviation GA).

One section of the tales deserves special comment, namely, the stories built around an item of material culture—the dumb-bull (see Appendix 1). Here no type or motif numbers are assigned, although the latter could properly be so designated. The distribution of the dumb-bull tradition does not seem to be very widespread, though references to such an item have been found in a few places. It is tempting to suggest that this collection of dumb-bull anecdotes is the most comprehensive study of such a tradition to date, but there may be studies unknown to this author. Tales in this tradition would probably be classed as local legends, even though the stories are beginning to show recurring patterns which border on fiction.

The heritage of some of the tales is certainly international in scope and probably pre-Christian in age. Some of the numskull stories, for example, date back to Buddhist birth stories and even to Hinduism. One church-related tale, "Dividing the Souls" (tale 28), has been traced back to an A.D. 593 Latin text (see note to this tale). And, of course, with most of the tales there is a close correspondence between Old World and the New World traditions, such as in the witch tales. The dumb-bull tradition itself, so long thought to be of local—or certainly Southern— heritage, may *perhaps* be linked with puberty rites in New Guinea and Australia.

Yet within the tales themselves are interwoven strands of local history and settings which give verity to the narration. All collectors of folklore quickly become aware of the artistry of the storyteller as he weaves traditional patterns of folklore into the framework of his own community. The tale may incorporate the setting of old Pisgah Cemetery in Grady County or a local character such as the Harrison boy or Sol Whitfield. Even if historical names and places are not given, traditions may be used to lend credence to the tale. One tradition, for example, that was part of the county in the early 1900s was an annual pilgrimage to the coast (around Panacea or Shell Point, Florida) to buy salt fish (for a detailed study of this tradition see Introduction). Two tales relate specifically to this practice: a supernatural tale by Allen Womble, "Ghost of a Baby" (tale 2), and a tall tale written by M. P. Maxwell, "Mule Almost Drowns in Mud-hole" (tale 45).

This collection of tales corroborates once again the commonly held assumption that folklore is the mirror of culture, reflecting not just historical settings and traditions, but strengths and weaknesses of a people as well. The Southern rural life in the early twentieth century, with its slow, plodding pace, its economic life subject to the whims and caprices of weather, bred men and women of strength who were yet somewhat stoical in their outlook. They accepted without question the need for collaborative efforts in assisting neighbors and even strangers in times of trouble and need. Children were taught, even in eating habits—children were served after adults when large crowds gathered—that others' needs came first. They also saw the need for religion as a staying force and the social activities perpetuated by the church as a buffer against the daily struggle to subsist. For work was hard, and times were tight. Southerners, in short, needed social contact—to talk, to eat, to laugh. Usually all three could be found through the church. And the hospitality attributed to the South in the past was not apocryphal; it existed and was extended even to travelers merely passing through. Such qualities were, and to a large extent still are, part of the South's strength. Many of these traits are evidenced in its folktales.

Isolation in the rural areas, however, bred other, less desirable traits—a narrowness, an inability to tolerate life-styles and races except in preconceived notions: the aim of each female was to secure a husband, and blacks were tolerated and even liked as long as they stayed in their place. These prejudices are, of course, part of the oral tradition, with some tales centering upon the old maids who resort to deceit to gain a mate and blacks who at times must be frightened into compliance. But the blacks, in turn, as evidenced by many of the numskull stories purported to be part of the black tradition, had their own scapegoat in the guise of the Irishman. In short, many of the humorous tales poke fun at not only blacks but Irishmen and traveling salesmen, people who were unacquainted with the ways of rural life in Georgia. The tales, however, are told in good fun and are seldom harsh or biting in their satire.

The traditional prose narrative, although remaining recognizable in form, is subject to changes both in the various milieus in which it travels and in its structural makeup as well. An Aesopian fable, such as "Bundle of Twigs" (tale 50), may move from its simple structure depicting the need for unity among family members to a more complex structure depicting the proper association of capital, labor, and organization (see version B of this tale). Some of the Grady County tales show the progress or re-

16

gression of a folktale as it makes it way into other folklore genres. Two of the tales, for example, have been used, in reduced states, as proverbs: the numbskull story "Carrying Part of the Load" (see note to tale 11), and the tall tale "Is the Corn Shucked?" (see note to tale 39). "The Obstinate Wife" (tale 49) has, according to Halpert, been reduced to a "Wellerism"—a kind of proverbial phrase (see note to this tale). And two other stories have gone through radical changes in structure through a long history of deleting, combining, or rearranging various motifs: "Ghost Scaring the Ghost" (see note to tale 26) and "Dividing the Souls" (see note to tale 28).

Some of the tales have been perpetuated through the printed word, for example in jestbooks, as well as through oral tradition (see "Carrying Part of the Load," tale 11, and "What Did Paul Say?" tale 29). Still others, such as "Dividing the Souls" (tale 28), "Nothing Except the Fence" (tale 47), and "Racing a Ghost" (tale 1), have not only been transmitted through the oral tradition but have been incorporated into other areas of the arts: song, verse, and drama (see headnotes to these tales for analyses). As stated at the outset of this study, tales may indeed experience addition, deletion, or synthesis—but, as long as they have life, never suffer from rigidity.

Three major indexes have been used in the classification of these tales: Stith Thompson's second revision and expansion of Antti Aarne's catalog of European folktale types, *The Types of the Folktale;* Stith Thompson's *Motif-Index of Folk Literature;* and Ernest W. Baughman's *Type and Motif Index of the Folktales of England and North America* (see Bibliography). Since these three works are so widely known by folklore students and are essential tools for classifying tales, I refer to their authors in the notes by last names only.

The tales themselves have been edited with an eye toward preserving textual accuracy as much as possible and are classified according to type and motif wherever relevant.

Introduction

Natives to southwest Georgia know that it is not the grandiose countryside filled with high drama and picture-postcard perfection which gives this area its appeal. These are the obvious signs which the entrepreneur or the politican looks for when selling an area to a large company or to tourists. What gives this area its appeal are the subtleties in landscape and even its imperfections, such imperfections as a Flannery O'Connor might hold up to kaleidoscopic review. A turn here, a turn there, and the eccentricities and imperfections mingle, fall away, mingle again. And finally, when all convergence seems impossible, the fragmented and distorted pieces fall into a pattern so harmonious that even the native Georgian is surprised by the uniqueness and beauty of this place and its inhabitants.

These subtle blendings might escape the average tourist bent upon traveling the bland interstate looking for only dramatic changes in landscape. But if he seeks out the small towns and rural sections of southwest Georgia, he will experience, along with the highly romanticized magnolias and mint juleps, the ubiquitous briers of the blackberry bush and the omnipresent ice-cold colas in the country stores. There are never-ending displays of contrasts—the sharp needles of the tall, splotchy slash pine intermingling with the intricately patterned leaf of the massive, softly spreading live oak. In the winter sunset, golden broom-straw stands in a derelict field near a newly planted crop of green oats or rye. And along a country road one discovers the wood-framed, unpainted shanty, complete with a washing machine on the porch and a tire hanging from a tree, down the road from a 1950s ranch-style brick house or a Tara-like, two-story white house with columns, verandah, and a trellis of pink roses.

Those who perceive beauty as only surface grandeur may not sing this land's glory, but those who see beauty as a mingling and play-off of opposites—juxtaposing the old with the new, the black with the white, the hills with the flatland, the rich with the poor, the sophisticate with the bumpkin—will be drawn to our land and will never be able to leave it altogether.

The seasonal changes themselves bear witness to south Georgia's understated beauty. There are not the dramatic changes that one would find even in north Georgia when the leaves of summer leap dramatically into bright, blazing reds and golds of fall. The change is so gradual that it is almost imperceptible. At some point near Thanksgiving the south Georgian begins to remark that fall has finally come when the trees grace the land with subtle shades of red and gold. Other changes are less obvious and hence more exquisite in their transformation from season to season. In the winter the ubiquitous kudzu, a vining plant brought into the state to control erosion, looms ominously like a capacious carpet of bleached bones, the warp and the woof of vines interwoven to suggest the carcasses of large animals laid to rest until spring. But with spring the bleached-out grayish white changes to mauve, forming a contrast to the newness of yellow-green grass along the south Georgia highways. And with the coming of summer the patterns of kudzu, in its full-blown stage, become larger-than-life works of art, sculptured by nature into massive elephants, giraffes, or prehistoric dinosaurs as the vines creep over abandoned cars or deserted houses and barns and climb telephone poles or trees.

Where the weather is concerned, there is a never-ending cycle of change. The south Georgian may be lulled into complacency and contentment by two weeks of uninterrupted sunshine and warmth only to be jarred into annoyance and irritation when the weather shifts into ten or twelve days of unending rain or mist. Even the warm, balmy summers of south Georgia become both blessing and nemesis to its inhabitants. Before the days of air conditioning, the summer months, although stirring images of warm, balmy weather, had their moments of extremes which south Georgians had to withstand. Early architectural styles reflect some of the area's solutions to the horrendous heat—long, wide central hallways running the length of the houses (called dog-trot houses) where cooling breezes could circulate over the entire house, and wide porches (some later screened to keep out mosquitoes, cockroaches, and chickens) providing areas for sitting, eating, entertaining, and even sleeping. On these hot days of summer with a humidity of 98 percent and a temperature of 102 degrees in the shade, the inhabitants of Georgia's southernmost counties find it incredible that the South ever rose again or was even able to rise the first time. The extreme heat can be at the least debilitating and at the most devastating; it is endured by south Georgians with steeled determination not to think about the temperature and with large supplies of tea, soft drinks, lemonade, and, for the good old boys, ice-cold beer.

Even with these extremes, the climate of south Georgia has been the means of surviving and even prospering economically. Such is the case, for example, with the counties of Thomas and Grady along the state's southern border. After the Civil War the South was floundering, trying to readjust to its losses, especially to the dethronement of one of its major economic resources—King Cotton. (Of course, this usurpation of cotton was assisted by a strong ally, the boll weevil, in the 1920s.) Thomas County, however, soon discovered that it had a gold mine in its climate alone, especially in the area around Thomasville. Robert C. Balfour, Jr., in his book on Thomasville and its environs, describes the awakening of the city to its potential for attracting tourists with its warm climate:

> Something occurred to change the entire outlook for the people of Thomasville and surrounding country. Sir William Osler, for many years a teacher of internal medicine at Johns Hopkins, in his famous textbook named the best climates for tuberculosis as Phoenix, Arizona; Saranac Lake, New York; and Thomasville, Georgia.
>
> The winter climate of Thomasville was much more pleasant than the other places suggested, so Thomasville developed rapidly. First, the boarding houses were filled with visitors who came for their health and sat in Paradise Park breathing the pure air from the pine tree area which seemed beneficial. Then the visitors discovered that the abandoned cotton fields were full of Bob White quail, and wealthy and prominent persons the nation over poured

Introduction

in to enjoy the hunting. (Robert C. Balfour, *This Land I Have Loved* [Tallahassee: Rose Printing Co., 1975], p. 66)

Large hotels, such as the Piney Woods and the Mitchell House, were subsequently built to accommodate these wealthy and prominent visitors. And large tracts of land were bought by well-educated Northerners such as "Jock" Whitney, ambassador to England and financier of the film *Gone with the Wind,* and Melville Hanna, brother to Senator Mark Hanna, industrialist and key advisor to President William McKinley (Senator Hanna did rent, however, a home in Thomasville, where he entertained Ohio governor and later President McKinley among many other visitors). Then and now this small southwest Georgia city, with its plantations and its beautiful and renowned roses, draws hundreds of visitors annually. Yet Thomasville seldom boasts of the many prominent figures who come there. The city seems to take it for granted that the wealthy and notable should gravitate to its life-style, especially those who seek the climate and the numerous outdoor sports which are available. So the prominent and celebrated are a part of Thomasville's heritage—Rockefeller, Eisenhower, William McKinley, Jackie Onassis, the duke and duchess of Windsor. These and many others have visited southwest Georgia frequently to spend leisure time enjoying friends, sports, and, above all else, the climate.

For surrounding areas in southwest Georgia, the climate has nurtured, along with tourism, a highly stable agricultural life as well. Having a long growing season (March through November) has granted the farmer much flexibility and diversity. Counties such as Grady, Thomas, Mitchell, and Decatur, whose economic survival has depended on agriculture, owe much to a climate which allowed them to diversify the types of crops grown. The emergence of this diversification, along with the enormous change in methods of farming brought about by increased mechanization, had a long and trying history. At the turn of the century cotton still reigned supreme as the number one money crop in southwest Georgia. This dependence upon cotton began to be questioned, however, with the advent of the boll weevil and later with the declining prices after World War I.

21

Introduction

Southwest Georgia farmers did not wait for doom to fall, for they had much earlier read the signs and had begun to employ more diversification in their crops. William Rogers maintains that in the 1890s Thomas County (Grady was then still part of Thomas) was the leader in the South in diversification.

> While Thomas County farmers were not on their way to an agricultural utopia, and they planted too much of their land in cotton, to an important degree they had diversified, reduced their cotton acreage, and were less dependent on cotton than other counties in Georgia and the South, . . . [because] Thomas County soil especially in the area around Cairo produced excellent crops of sugarcane. Farmers were quick to discover this, and cane molasses, or syrup as it was more frequently called, soon became an important part of the diet of the people. In 1860 Thomas County ranked third in the state behind Decatur and Brooks in the production of syrup. (William Rogers, *Thomas County, 1865–1900* [Tallahassee: Florida State University Press, 1973], p. 59)

And by the turn of the century interest in tobacco and pecan production was gaining momentum in the southwest Georgia area.

Through diversification and increased mechanization southwest Georgia farmers found their strength and staying power, and progress escalated by leaps and bounds. For this was a climate which did not demand procrustean adherence to just one major crop—it provided flexibility. At the beginning of the twenties Grady County was exemplary of the progress brought about by diversification. "Grady County has the reputation all over the country for being the only county in the state where diversification is practiced entirely. . . . Not content with being the largest pure sugar cane syrup market in the world, the county is rapidly forging to the front in the production of tobacco, livestock, corn, and pecans" (*Cairo Messenger*, 2 April 1920).

This ability to adapt and to endure regardless of hardships characterizes the Southern farmer, who with his devotion to the land, has had to embrace many changes and withstand numerous disasters. Grady County farmers in their sixties or seventies, such as my father, who began farming careers with the mule, the plow, and the wagon have had to make major adjustments in their thinking and planning just to survive. And the strength necessary to weather two world wars, the Great Depression, extreme poverty, and devastating epidemics of influenza is the kind of strength we usually attribute to our heroes. Yet such is the kind of heroism we find among the average older farmer in the county— in a Leroy Mann, for example, who lost two daughters, his mother, and his best mule within a four-month period.

Whether it is the climate, the hard agrarian life-style, or even the beating that the South took during the Civil War, many factors have contributed to the character of the people in this area. And it is in the character of the people that south Georgia's uniqueness lies. The great Henry W. Grady, Georgia's quixotic prophet-orator and editor of the *Atlanta Constitution* during the 1880s (also the man for whom Grady County is named), told a tale which inadvertently delineated the people in southwest Georgia with their imposing natures:

> There was an old preacher once who told some boys of the Bible lesson he was going to read in the morning. The boys, finding the place, glued together the connecting pages. The next morning he read on the bottom of one page, "When Noah was one hundred and twenty years old he took unto himself a wife, who was"—then turning the page—"140 cubits long—40 cubits wide, built of gopher wood—and covered with pitch inside and out." He was naturally puzzled at this. He read it again, verified it, and then said, "My friends, this is the first time I ever met this in the Bible, but I accept this as an evidence of the assertion that we are fearfully and wonderfully made." (Henry W. Grady, *The New South: Writings and Speeches of Henry Grady* [Savannah: Beehive Press, 1971], p. 4)

Stories abound in south Georgia communities about these people who are "fearfully and wonderfully made," people who cannot be categorized or pigeonholed, who loom as rugged individualists or "characters." In rural, conservative communities where values seem to be locked up tightly and generally agreed upon, there is, oddly enough, not only a tolerance but even a fascination for such characters, tales of whom are passed down from generation to generation.

There are stories of Rit Hayes, who was haunted by visitations of his dead wife; of Marcel White, whose humorous quips made him the Will Rogers of his community; of Aaron Bodiford, the hermit who carried a sack of bottles on his back and became the object of fascination for many small children (who were under the apprehension that the sack contained bad children, especially those who talked back to their parents).

One story of two such unusual characters revolved around a local Methodist church, two antithetical religious views, and a surprisingly harmonious conclusion. The story went like this. Sister Molly Pelham, a very pious and upstanding woman in a local rural Methodist church, was renowned for her ability to pray. And almost every Sunday she was called upon by Preacher Taylor to lead the congregation "to the throne of grace." Outside of the confines of the church lived a notorious, self-proclaimed atheist, called simply by the name of Old Man Mac, who just happened to own a farm which adjoined the church property (this particular church was in actuality a small square-framed house just behind the country store). Old Man Mac, it was said, many times took great delight in confronting "Miss Molly" with his blasphemies, to which, it was said, Miss Molly would respond by dropping to her knees in front of him, lifting her head and hands simultaneously toward heaven, and praying for the deliverance of his heavily threatened soul.

One particular summer a heat wave settled over southwest Georgia, bringing with it temperatures of 103 degrees with 100 percent humidity, parched lands and crops, and one of the longest droughts ever seen in the county. A special service was subsequently called by the Methodists to pray for rain to end the drought. People gathered for an afternoon prayer sesson. There was singing and praying, followed by sermonettes, more singing, and finally more praying. For this last supplication for the rain, the best and most powerful "pray-ers" had been summoned. Miss Molly, of course, was among them. Old Man Mac, however, up to his usual devilment of the believers, had positioned himself on a large stump near the open side-windows of the church. As the prayers inside were commencing, Old Man Mac began to utter his blasphemies and his remonstrances against a god who would withhold the rain. Simultaneously, Preacher Taylor, having

heard these blasphemies, decided to bring out his big gun—
namely, Sister Molly. He announced in an angry, booming voice
as he looked out the window: "Sister Molly, would you please
lead us to the throne of glory and save us from this community
blight which is bringing this cursed drought!" Miss Molly began
her prayer, reaching a crescendo as she moved nearer and nearer
the window. Floating in the windows on this hot afternoon came
the loud words of the blasphemer as he shouted toward heaven:
"You ole ████████████████, why cain't ya send the rains!"

The accused words shocked the assemblage but brought resolu-
tion from Miss Molly. Resounding against the walls of the church
and rebounding out of the windows into the open field came Miss
Molly's resonant and deep voice: "Oh, dear God, we ask that you
forgive this blasphemer, ignore his sins, and send the rains upon
us! We ask it in thy name. Amen. Amen."

And as the two pleas clashed and collided in their ascent heav-
enward, the lightning split the skies, the thunder rumbled across
the heavens, and the rain poured in torrents on the parched
ground. It was long pondered and debated in the county whether
it was Old Man Mac's chastisement of God or Miss Molly's plea
for rain and forgiveness which brought the rains.

Such a story, although greatly embellished through repeated
tellings, brings together certain extremes which do exist in southwest Georgia—not only the extremes of climate but those which
exist among the people of the area. As a native of Grady County,
Georgia, I feel that I can look both realistically and idealistically
at a people who are indeed "fearfully and wonderfully made." I
have not always been proud of being a Southerner when the
media, especially television, depicts us as being red-necked and
semi-illiterate. Perhaps our manner of speaking slowly and drawing out our vowels has contributed to this image along with our
slow manner of moving (perhaps due to the extreme heat and the
high humidity). But even I am constantly amazed at the level of
sophistication found here, both in intellect and in the culture.
Having taught in the secondary and collegiate schools of this area
for two decades, I have seen extraordinarily fertile minds, occasionally bordering on genius, pass through our classrooms. Some
of our high school students have attended and ultimately gradu-

ated from such universities as Emory, University of North Carolina, Vanderbilt, Columbia, and Yale. In the debate world alone Grady County has in the past produced speakers who received national acclaim for excellence and went on to become outstanding leaders in forensics at leading universities.

Where the people are concerned, there certainly seems to be an inherent sophistication which is passed on from generation to generation. So many native south Georgians seem to have excellent taste in clothes, in decorating, in landscaping—a feel and a flair for creation, whether it be in sewing clothes, preparing and serving food, designing a home or church, or growing flowers. Above all, there is an awareness of others and hence a graciousness in meeting and dealing with human beings, whether next-door neighbors or total strangers. If the true sophisticate is one who has a heightened awareness of life and of humanity in general and has a wish to put others at their ease, then there are many sophisticates in this region.

The question may be asked, "But what about the uneducated and the prejudices and intolerances shown by the racial bigot and the religious zealot, all of which abound in south Georgia?" Yes, there are extremes in this area—the student who, in his senior year, can barely read above the sixth-grade level; the poorly spoken English with traces of the old Anglo-Saxon verbs (He *holped* build this church); the social separation of the black and white communities; and the intolerance and narrow-mindedness springing from religious fundamentalism. These shortcomings are still with us even though they are not as great as they were in the past. Many of these failings have perhaps been aggravated by an insularity produced by a predominantly agrarian lifestyle. With all of the religious influence in the South, it also seems paradoxical that we are simultaneously known for our extreme prejudice. But even here the prejudice is juxtaposed with tolerance and even magnanimity. There certainly are the social prejudices between whites and blacks, yet now as in the past there are great friendships which exist across the races. Even so, the prejudicial heritage is something which we would like to bury or at least put behind us. Most educated Southerners have come to see the absurdity of the traditions in the past: that a black man had access to the occupants of a white household only through the back door, that blacks and whites never ate at the same table or the same restaurant, that no black ever sat beside a white on the bus (a custom humorously but poignantly portrayed by the great Georgia writer, Flannery O'Connor, in the short story "Everything That Rises Must Converge"), or that whites and blacks never drank from the same water fountain or shared the same rest room. Although segregation within the churches remains inviolable (except for funerals, weddings, and occasional random visits), the schools were integrated in the late sixties without undue incidents although the county had fought earlier against desegregation. In this struggle, however, Grady County never did threaten to close down its system in retaliation as did many other counties in Georgia. Though some people in the area remain prejudiced, others are enlightened and even tolerant now, and the county as a whole is actively seeking to ensure equality under the law if not socialization between the races. We would hope, as Matthew Arnold advocated when assessing the age of the witch trials, that future generations will view the South in context, noting its ingrained life-styles and beliefs, and look a little more tolerantly upon us and our deeds.

All of these extremes and incongruities in our landscape, climate, educational background, and people intermingle, fall away, intermingle again—each holding its place in the Southern tradition.

Even this word tradition—the stuff of which stories are made and the stuff with which true Southeners are inundated—seems almost an anachronism in a modern society, as does the South itself. For the American society is one which prides itself on rapid change, movement, and newness, all of which are justified and even exonerated in the name of "progress." But in the South, certainly the South I knew as a child, tradition reigned supreme. These traditions were not learned from books or television but were passed on by word of mouth from one generation to another. Traditions of manners, food preparation, churchgoing, land preparation, etc., were taught along with interracial and sexual mores and family obligations. The native south Georgian is so steeped in these traditions that he is astounded to learn that in other parts of the country people do not wave to strangers; say "yes, ma'am" and "no, ma'am" to parents, teachers, and older adults; offer blessings over each meal; think that "y'all" is the only plural of "you"; and stay loyal to family members through thick and thin. In the foreword to *A History of Georgia*, which he commissioned while governor of the state, President Jimmy Carter, in stating some of his own affinities for Georgia, characterized much about native Georgians in general: "This family and community spirit was essential to Georgia's early settlers. This same spirit has withstood the test of time and circumstance. We were able to make it through the Revolutionary and Civil Wars and still retain many of our original values and traditions."[1]

These values and traditions are perpetuated by and evidenced in the institutions of the church and the family. Both loom, especially in the past, as inviolable behemoths against which no questions are directed and no attacks levelled. Both are, in short, sacrosanct to the typical Southerner.

The church, be it Baptist (Primitive, or Hard Shell, and missionary Baptists), Methodist, or Presbyterian, is the home away from home, the center for numerous social activities, and, of course, the bedrock upon which the religious faith is built and enacted. It is here that economic and social lines are crossed, interwoven, and blended as the poor meet the rich, the uneducated encounter the educated, and the young interact with the old.

Traditional in most churches are annual revivals (called protracted meetings in earlier times) and "dinner-on-the-grounds." It is usually in the spring or summer that revivals are held, sometimes for one week, occasionally for two. A minister from the "outside" is brought in, one who is known more as a "preacher" than as a teacher. For a strong oratorical talent can awaken lethargic church members and provide the impetus for at least "rededicating" their lives to God and, at most, saving their souls by making "a profession of faith" and joining the church. Music is a

1. Jimmy Carter, foreword, *A History of Georgia*, ed. Kenneth Coleman et al. (Athens: University of Georgia Press, 1977), p. xiii.

large part of the atmosphere (except with Primitive Baptists, who renounce musical instruments and use only the voice—a practice followed by the Sacred Harp Singers), especially the great old hymns such as "Amazing Grace" or "Just as I Am." When the audience sings softly, "Oh Lamb of God, I come, I come," as someone comes down to the altar to "begin his life in Christ," there is much emotion.

Occasionally on Sundays at noon the entire congregation of a church might "spread dinner" together, thereby creating a veritable feast of traditional Southern foods—fried chicken, roast beef, cream-style corn, white-acre peas, butter beans, chicken pie, apple cobbler, a twelve-layer cake with chocolate icing. The list is endless. In the past the food was frequently spread on wire stretched over wood bracing. The picnic table, sinking in the middle with the weight of the food, might measure fifty feet or more in length and still be inadequate to hold all the varied dishes. Such occasions for eating and talking were and are memorable indeed, celebrating communal sharing and the exchange of ideas or stories from the past.

The family, like the church, is no less cohesive, fostering much devotion, especially in years past. Then the family was large, frequently numbering ten or more children. These children, when grown, would seldom leave the vicinity, for family ties were close and quite binding. For many, family life was and is, all in all, sufficient unto itself. Frequently, family members "when grown and married" may choose to build their homes down the road or across from the parents, thereby interacting and eating with them almost daily (or certainly on Sundays). These large extended families, although generating some problems through too much closeness, do, however, produce a sense of stability and ongoingness in this highly transient modern world in which we live. In short, the child grows up knowing that he is cared about by many relatives, not just those of the immediate family. With this caring comes a heightened sense of responsibility to and for the family, a sense that one's behavior (either good or bad) affects many others in the family unit.

These institutions, along with many other customs of the

South, do breed special kinds of people and a unique life-style. Those who leave the South frequently return home; if they do not return, they send remonstrances back to family members reminding them of the rich quality of life that they have here. All, of course, is not perfection in this Southern Eden, for the inconsistencies, the incongruities, the extremes, and the hardships remain even in this modern age. When these variances, however, converge, fall away, and intermingle once again, the blending brings forth a most exquisitely beautiful land and people, a people strong in their faith and courage, deserving to be emulated by generations to come.

Social Functions of the Tales

The functions of folklore are diverse in nature; social needs for tales are as varied as the cultures from which they emerge. Vagabonds from Russia may use folktales to secure food and lodging (Thompson, *The Folktale*, p. 451); settlers in Kakasd (southern Hungary), to ease the tediously long hours of a funeral wake or deathwatch;[2] still others, simply to entertain during leisure hours. Alan Dundes, in his introduction to William Bascom's article "Four Functions of Folklore," admonishes folklore collectors to record sociocultural contexts as well as the specific item of folklore: "One cannot always tell from form alone what the associated contextual function is. Functional data must, therefore, be recorded when the item is collected. An item once removed from its social context and published in this way deprives the scientific folklorist of an opportunity to understand why the particular item was used in the particular situation to meet a particular need."[3]

Folktales in Grady County have been used in the past pri-

2. Linda Dégh, "Some Questions of the Social Functions of Storytelling," *Acta Ethnographica* 6 (1957–58): 118.

3. Alan Dundes, *The Study of Folklore* (Englewood Cliffs, New Jersey: Prentice Hall), p. 279.

marily to make work easier and to provide entertainment during leisure hours. As the county is predominantly an agricultural community, most of the tales come from and reflect the rural area where, before the age of great mechanization, work was arduous and long, frequently involving communal efforts to complete a task. In addition to collecting folktales from a given region, the folklorist should also seek to establish these contextual functions of the tales, both in the past and in the present.

The places where folktales are told in Grady County seem to be narrowing considerably as conditions and social needs within the area change. In the early part of this century before families owned automobiles, which raced over the countryside, or televisions, which dominated leisure time, the need for social interchange was much greater than now. Most work or even pleasurable activities were group orientated, thereby furnishing a ready audience for the storyteller. When the storytellers—all of whom were over fifty years of age—were interviewed and asked where they learned their stories, most of them cited situations which are no longer common today. Aside from hearing stories in the home around the fireside, storytellers gathered many tales during trips to Shell Point, Florida, to buy salt fish; while performing communal work on the county roads; and in the course of agricultural work, related especially to tobacco and sugar cane. Some historical analysis, therefore, of the social background seems pertinent, for this particular body of folktales speaks to and reflects these earlier times.

One unique occasion for storytelling in Grady County in the early part of this century was a two- or three-day journey to Shell Point, Florida, to buy salt fish. This trek to the coast in covered wagons ostensibly was to buy seafood to carry the family through the winter; to the travelers, and especially to the children, however, the journey was an anticipated adventure. Mr. Irven Singletary, a Cairo resident before his death in 1977, recalled that fish were never sold for less than fifty cents a dozen in the county.[4] If a

4. Interview with Mr. Irven Singletary, July 1972. An ad was carried in the *Cairo Messenger*, August 21, 1908: "Salt Fish for sale by the hundred or barrel . . . Ashmore, Florida."

family went down to the coast, they got their dried fish and roe for almost nothing. And they had salt fish throughout the winter (even sometimes until May), enough for sharing with neighbors or selling to the "hands" on the farm.

William W. Rogers, in *Thomas County, 1865–1900*, notes that this practice was in existence in neighboring Thomas County in the last of the nineteenth century:

> It is clear that such trips were not limited to the affluent. Annual trips to the coast were made by entire country families. After the crops were gathered, a farmer would convert his wagon into a traveling tent, make a place in the rear for cooking utensils, collect his family, and head for the bay. There was no hurry, and as the wagon creaked southward the family dogs (and other pets) provided escort. At twilight the day's journey ended, and the evening campfire, even when difficult to light, was looked forward to. (Pp. 250–51)

Descriptions of preparation for the journey were even more explicitly given by Mr. Singletary:

> We'd put a cover over the wagon, high enough so that you could stand up in it. Then we'd put slats across the floor of the wagon, and our springs and bedding would go on top of these. Under the slats would go our feed for the mules. We then had us a trough on the back of the wagon for them to eat out of. We next carried us plenty of food—boiled ham, side meat, meal, flour and syrup. Sometimes we'd carry a chicken, but it had to be alive, because it wouldn't keep long. Only one or two of us children got to go each year because there just wasn't enough room in the wagon. (Interview, July 1972)

The feed for the mules also served at times as bedding for the children, according to Mr. Alto Sellers. The parents slept on the bed inside the wagon; the children, on bedrolls or fodder, under the wagon. "Along in those days we'd share fodder; say, if we didn't have enough bedrolls, we'd share a fodder. And then us younguns would put a quilt on that and lay on it" (interview, September 11, 1975).

Usually the wagon train (several families or one family with many relatives) would stop at least twice to spend the night before reaching Shell Point, perhaps at Wakulla, Bradfordville, or Tallahassee. And even Tallahassee, as Edna Hall recalls, "was nothing. To me it didn't look as big as Cairo, but it surely must have been. . . . But it just wasn't anything but a stop in the road" (interview, August 29, 1976).

Mrs. Hall dated one excursion around 1915 and reminisced about one special night at the campsite:

> I remember them feeding me and the cousin that was younger than me in the wagon that night, because the mosquitoes were so bad. And I can remember walking out in the water while the tide was low—with a board. We had some big, old, red Georgia Thumpers—two-, three-inch grasshoppers—on the board. We'd set them on the board and take them out in the water and ride them. They wouldn't jump off in the water, you see. (Interview, August 29, 1976)

Mr. Elmer Wilcox, coroner of Grady County, elaborated on the storytelling and "frolicking" that took place at the campsites:

> It's what, about thiry-fives miles to Tallahassee? . . . But, anyway, that's where they fed the horses that night. Then they'd build a big old fire out there in the middle and pull out them old guitars and fiddles; they'd just about keep us awake all night. . . . Well, they say people came from everywhere round there to gather up; that was their gathering place in the fall of the year in October. And they'd swap yarns. (Interview, August 3, 1976)

Elaborating on the yarn swapping, Mr. Wilcox filled in details about the whole storytelling process, one which seems Chaucerian in framework:

> There was a lot of them old stories, but I was too small to remember a lot of them. But I can remember them just laughing and having a big time and telling those tales. And when they got through, they'd all vote to see who was the best tale teller. . . . Of course, they didn't have news media and all that to take it out, but the word would get around you know, that old Joe, he was the best tale teller. (Interview, August 3, 1976)

All was not pleasure, however, in this seacoast excursion, for much work awaited the travelers at Shell Point unless they were wealthy enough to hire the work done. Mr. Wilcox explained that procedure following the last night of camping:

> Then the next morning, at the crack of day, they'd hitch up those mules to their wagons and go on to the coast. They'd carry those big, old oak barrels down there, and they'd buy those fish there. They'd split them, salt them down, and bring them back for the whole neighborhood up there. You know, everybody had fish when they came back, 'cause that's what they went for. If they didn't have money, you know, they'd swap meat and syrup and lard—whatever they had—for the fish down there. (Interview, August 3, 1976)

Mr. M. P. Maxwell acknowledged the use of storytelling on the pilgrimage to Shell Point but maintained that another very important avenue for the transmission of tales was road-working details in the county.

> This road work produced a variety of things. It brought together friends and enemies and gave a chance to talk, listen, and laugh. It also had its share of fistfights; it gave some an audience to quote Scripture. To others it gave a chance to release some of their vast knowledge about politics, farming, and personal stories they contained, to the point of talk or bust. (Interview, August 13, 1972)

A man named George, Mr. Maxwell recalled, told marvelous tall tales while (or instead of) working.

Prior to the use of convict labor and, ultimately, modern road machinery, men in the community, through communal labor, kept the dirt roads operable. Mr. Maxwell explained the system:

> The public roads were kept open and passable for wagons and buggies by those farm men and their help. Every male between the ages of sixteen and fifty years old were subject to road work which usually was done about twice each year.[5] It was supposed to be a time when it would be of least interference with planting and harvesting. This time was at the discretion of the road commissioner and the overseer. . . . The overseer would write out summons or send word orally. If one wanted to renege by saying he

5. Mr. Maxwell's statistics here are corroborated by William W. Rogers in *Thomas County, 1865–1900*, p. 99.

didn't get the word, they saw that he got a summons, and a bailiff was put over him to see he did work, such as digging stumps, or a harder task. (Interview, August 13, 1972)

Although allowances were made for those who were sick or physically disabled, much inequity existed in the system. A letter published in the *Cairo Messenger* (August 25, 1911) attesting to the inequities and asking support for road taxation was written by P. H. Ward:

> An Overseer summons out his hands, it matters not how important it may be that he should attend to some other business on that day. He must lay it aside and go or pay a fine. When he gets there, a few men in the squad do the work, the others stand around and talk and idle away the time. Tax every man subject to a road duty and the burden falls on all alike. Again a squad of men with weeding hoes and a Dixie plow cannot work a road to any advantage as compared with improved road machinery.

In Mr. Maxwell's day the idler would probably be a fellow like George who entertained his co-workers with his unbelievable yarns. In any event, Mr. Maxwell, who worked in his father's place before he became sixteen, said that although he worked hard, he thoroughly enjoyed the storytellers.

Linda Dégh in her analysis of the social function of folktales in Hungary listed among other contexts the importance of the agricultural-proletarian working communities in the development of the European folktales. "Tales are learnt and told at the places of work, outside the village, and the character of the job determines the manner in which tales are told. . . . Almost any kind of trivial and not excessively exacting work in the fields may offer opportunities to listen to tales where they have a refreshing effect" ("Social Functions of Storytelling," p. 107). It seems that agriculture creates many common bonds with other peoples of the world. People who work with the land, regardless of nationality, live with the uncertainty of the elements and the disappointment and devastation that bad crop years can bring. Before the advent of modern machinery, the work was hard, long, and tiring. Hence, as Dégh suggests, the opportunity for storytelling lessened the tedious, tiresome work and brought refreshment.

Introduction

Certainly, such was true in Grady County in the day of the mule and plow, before mechanization.

Two kinds of work most frequently mentioned by the narrators as being conducive to storytelling were the processing of tobacco and the making of syrup from sugarcane. Whether it was large families working cooperatively, neighbors exchanging work, or simply hired hands working for money, both crops involved large numbers of people in communal activities. Syrup making had long been a tradition in most rural families, but tobacco production was just coming into its own. A promotional article in the *Cairo Messenger* on March 22, 1907, championed the growth of sugarcane and tobacco: "The chief money crops being sugar cane, which they grow very extensively, there being something like 10,000 barrels marketed from this county every year, and which is claimed to be the finest in taste and flavor of any syrup manufactured in the state. Tobacco, while yet in its infancy, is fast becoming one of the leading money crops in the county, as the crop sells readily in the northern markets."

The small farmer was dedicated to growing enough sugarcane to furnish his family with syrup through the year; if there was syrup left over, then he would sell the surplus. The families who did not own their own syrup mill could work out exchanges with a nearby neighbor to have their cane ground. Syrup, as standard fare for dessert, was served in many families three times a day. And children usually packed a biscuit and a bottle of syrup in their lunch pails. Or they punched a hole in their biscuit before leaving home and filled the hole with syrup.

Cane was ground in the fall of the year when days were cool. People from nearby towns or other states came to cane grindings, where they could watch syrup being made, chat and share stories, drink cold cane juice from a common dipper, and buy home-made syrup. Mr. Early Gandy, a native farmer in the county, described the syrup-making process from the cane field through the cooking-out stage:

We usually hired someone to get the cane out, strip and top it. We usually got that done for a dollar a barrel. Cut it, pile it, and haul it to the mill. In the beginning we had two mules, a one-horse

36

wagon, and we'd haul it with the wagon. We'd fill up the rack at the mill—usually take one load. Then we'd go back and get another load while this mule was grinding what we called a "boiling" of syrup. We were cooking on the kettle at that time; the kettle would hold one hundred gallons of juice. We'd get about four or five boilings a day, depending upon how early we got to work that morning. If it was four o'clock, we could usually quit by dark and have about five boilings that day. Of course, we had to tote the pummies [ground cane stalks—pomace] off by hand, put them in a cotton basket, and carry them to the pummy pile. . . . We'd start in the morning about four o'clock. All the lights we had, besides a lantern or two, were some small fires. Under the syrup shelter was a scaffold built up. On that we burned lightwood splinters to make a light. Had a piece of metal for the wood to lay on. When we'd need a light somewhere else, we'd take a splinter burning and build another one.

We cooked the juice in a kettle. When we'd begin to heat it, we'd get the skimmings off. Then we'd set what we called a rim on the inside and let it boil up and run over that rim. Between that rim and the rim of the kettle there would be about four to six inches. We had a little skimmer, and we'd take the skimmings off with that.[6] At that time we didn't have any syrup tester. We had to make it by guess. My daddy was real good at that. He'd take his dipper up there, and it'd begin to flick off. Time to come out of there. We'd take the fire out with a long-handled hoe—a green one—so it wouldn't burn up. Cooled it off. Then get the syrup up and pour it into a half barrel and strain it up. One hundred gallons of juice would make about fifteen gallons of syrup if it was good sweet cane. The syrup was finally sealed in thirty-gallon barrels. That was a standard barrel. And they made barrels right here in Cairo, Cannon's Barrel Factory, located back of Wight's in Pierce's old warehouse. (Interview, July 25, 1976)

6. These skimmings were frequently made into "cane buck." Many jokes were made about the liquor's being so strong it would make you buck. The procedure was relatively simple: the skimmings were placed in an open-topped barrel with a bunghole near the bottom and allowed to sit overnight. The next morning one could take the peg out of the bunghole and draw off light-yellow sweet beer. The beer could then be placed in another barrel, with sugar or syrup added for sweetening, and allowed to work off about a month. The more times this procedure was repeated, the stronger the buck. Frequently, the buck (actually rum) was used in making moonshine whiskey.

During the cooking process was the time most conducive to chatting and storytelling. Around sunset or first dark in this dim light of lanterns and splinters the arduous day seemed softened. And even the "pummy" pile had a tradition of its own, a place where children came to play by day and lovers met to court by night. As Mr. Gandy explained, "They [children] played on the pummy pile, neighbor's children, too. The young people would court on it, too, get some cane and chew cane together—not much light there after dark, you know."[7]

The tobacco business was also on the upswing around Cairo after the turn of the century. A brief announcement appeared in the *Cairo Messenger* on January 11, 1907: "Mr. Henry Maxwell of Pine Hill, another tobacco man, has moved to town to engage in the tobacco business. Cairo is moving mightily in the direction of the 'filthy weed.'"

From the preparation of the tobacco bed in December to the gathering and cooking of the matured plant in June, many laborious hours were involved. Mr. Alto Sellers, a tobacco grower for over twenty years, recounts the procedure used in gathering the crop.

> We used to gather it by hand. We'd carry four rows. Four men would take a row apiece, and they would crop it by hand and then lay it in layers in the slide [sled]. The mule would then pull that slide from the patch to the barn. Sometimes there would be several mules and slides. At the barn they'd empty the slides; the womenfolks and the children would hand it and string it onto sticks. There would be somebody there then to go load the sticks in the barn. But way before that, you'd get into fighting hornworms and things of that kind. . . . It would then take about five days to cook it out. Once you started cooking back then, you always had to keep the furnace going. Then later on people found out there wasn't no need to cook it at night and began to quit it. When night come, they cooled down and went in the house and went to bed. But I never did do it; I set up, yeah, cooked mine off, and that way I got through with it a couple days earlier than they did.

7. Personal interview with Early and Lilly Gandy, July 25, 1976. Several of the narrators indicated that the "pummies" could be used for bedding in the barn lot or after rotting, for fertilizer for sweet potatoes.

After it cooked, you'd cool [it] down whenever you got the stems killed. Then you'd open the vents and the doors and let it get in case—limber it up to where you could handle it. How long that took depended on the conditions of the weather. If it was dry, a lot of times you'd have to haul water and pour in the barn [some moisture is necessary for the tobacco to get in case]. When it gets in case, you take it off them sticks and pile it up. Put it in sheets or either put it in them slides and carry it to wherever you want to pack it up. You can pack it up in windrows and put the tips together, or you can put it on sheets and go around and around with it. Sometimes then it'd be a month before you'd sell it, sometimes just one or two days. It just depended on the time that we had. You know tobacco will age. Most all tobacco used to when I first started, was shipped in hogsheads—big barrels. Whenever you went to the tobacco warehouse with it for auction, and you sold it, why you were done with it then. (Interview, September 11, 1975)

Anytime there were spare moments in the process was a good time for storytelling—waiting at the barn for a slide of tobacco, taking a break at lunch, but especially cooking out the tobacco. In earlier days when the cooking was done with a wood furnace, the farmer thought it necessary, as Mr. Sellers stated, to keep the heat up throughout the night. Someone, therefore, had to "sit up" at the barn to stoke the fire. Family or friends might stay with the farmer at least part of the night, especially if foods, such as chicken and rice, were brought in. Such a setting, with light from the lanterns and the occasional opening of the furnace door, was made to order for stories, especially ghost stories.

These social settings, mentioned by the storytellers themselves, are merely suggestive of places where folktales were perpetuated. Stories could be told wherever people gathered—church functions, barbershops, country stores, funeral wakes, fish frys—and whenever there was a storyteller present. The folktale in Grady County, although primarily used for entertainment, functioned possibly as a means of venting prejudices in a fairly harmless way, both for the whites and for the blacks. There is much frightening of the blacks and placing them in ludicrous positions in these folktales. But, likewise, there is the Irish scapegoat perpetuated in black lore.

39

The function of the tales transmitted today is still basically to entertain, even though life is not so strenuous as it was in the past. One wonders, however, if an additional function of the folklore now is not to acquaint the young with a culture that is past. When Mr. Glenn, for example, in establishing the setting for "Racing a Ghost," explains that there were neither hotels nor motels in that day, he is acquainting his audience with prior conditions in rural Georgia.

As to the transmission of the tales in the county today, much of it is done in homes at family gatherings. And even that seems to be waning with the rapidly changing life-styles. The communal activities are almost nonexistent now with the advent of scientific farming and highly mechanized equipment. Syrup is produced, not by the small farmer, but by large companies such as Roddenbery's in Cairo. Tobacco gathering is done now by tobacco harvesters and the cooking in galvanized sheet-metal barns with fancy thermostats. A trip to Shell Point in a wagon has been replaced by a jaunt down to the Zippy Mart in a Toyota Corona. And little dirt roads wide enough for mules and wagons have been superseded by four-lane superhighways.

Mrs. Edna Hall summarized the changes that have altered life not only in Grady County but everywhere:

> We got so commercialized that you could buy all the services that you needed, and you used to couldn't. . . . And so, you helped each other, and that's what we lost. . . . We just go and hire the funeral home to take over everything when somebody dies today. . . . It just wasn't available then, and everybody was closer together because the people needed help. And now about the only time you can help at a funeral . . . is to just feed the family. (Interview, August 29, 1976)

As to the future of this particular body of folklore, it is difficult to determine. If within families where these stories were transmitted there are storytellers, then perhaps they will continue to be perpetuated orally. If not, and with less time and fewer opportunities to tell tales, they could die out. Linda Dégh concludes: "Conception, form, and style of the folktale are all determined by the conditions in which it is born, and the tale will survive as long as these conditions prevail. Its development, flourishing,

Introduction

decay, and fluctuations follow the changes in social conditions" ("Social Functions of Storytelling," p. 91). Certainly many of the social conditions under which these tales were perpetuated have altered considerably. Folklore of some kind will always be transmitted; whether it will be this body of lore remains to be seen.

The Storytellers

William Robert Glenn

Any small gathering of people will probably bring forth a series of stories from the past if Mr. William Robert Glenn is in the gathering. For he has been telling tales for forty or fifty years, first to his own immediate family, then to his children, and now to his grandchildren.

If one asks him where he learns his stories, he answers, "Oh, here and there, from different people." But eventually he will tell you that he heard many of his tales when he was a boy at such an event as the fall cane grinding when it was syrup-making time. People would come from miles around to drink cold cane juice straight from the mill and to tell tales while the syrup was cooking. Or some of his tales came from nights of sitting up late at tobacco barns, tending the wood-heated furnace so that the tobacco could cook properly. Because "sitting up" was frequently an all-night process, relatives and friends oftentimes gathered to keep the person company at least during the early part of the night. Here was a perfect setting for storytelling, especially for some good ghost tales, where the only lights against the dark night were lanterns and the glow from the furnace. Thus Mr. Glenn was the recipient of many excellent stories from the past and has been the means of their being told time and time again to two succeeding generations.

Cane grindings and wood-heated tobacco barns are only a part of his farming experience, for he has been working with the land since he was a small boy and, hence, has seen the world of the

41

farmer change drastically. Born in 1908, Mr. Glenn grew up in rural Grady County where tractors were still pretty much unheard of and much of the farmwork was done with mules or horses. Even as a young man, married and with four daughters, he still worked part of the land with mule and plow. So he has had to learn new and better ways of farming to adapt himself to the rapid changes in farming technology during the last thirty years.

Although he worked for about a fifteen-year interval managing A&P grocery stores, he has always been first and last the farmer, loving the land and prizing the means of working the land— whether it was his mules in the early days or his Ford tractor in his later years. His family laughs to see the thirty-one-year-old Ford tractor still being used to work the garden; he retired from working his two farms in 1976. The little tractor that he loves is as much a part of him as his turtle-shell hat which he still claims is the coolest one made. Even while his family may smile at the picture he makes on his tractor, they are also very much aware of the exactness and precision with which he handled his farming, of the pride that he took in producing every year some of the finest crops in the county.

And, likewise, his stories are as much a part of him as farming and his family. And there never seems to be an end to the number that he knows. His ghost tales and "Pat and Mike" stories are still some of the favorite ones with the family. Many have been told so often that the grandchildren know when he changes any of the wording and immediately proceed to correct him. But at times even his family is shocked when after all these years of telling his famous Irishmen jokes of Pat and Mike, he suddenly introduces a completely new one. And you find yourself straining to hear what the new one will be when he says excitedly, "And, by shot, Pat said to Mike . . ."

Allen Womble

"There are some people who can tell a joke, and there's nothing to it; yet another fellow can tell the same joke, and Lord-a-mercy, you just bust yor sides a-laughing. And the more you think about it, the funnier it gets."

Frequently, a person very innocently captures in one statement much of the essence of what he himself is. Mr. Allen Womble has done just that in his statement on the art of joke telling. For he is indeed a man who knows how to tell a tale or relate a personal incident in his life so that it stays long with the listener. And the listener comes to be caught up with this man who needs no ludicrous situation to bring tears of laughter. All he needs is each day bringing its own little inconsistencies or absurdities and his family and friends around him in his work. And humor is everywhere.

He tells with much amusement even of his harrowing encounter with an old sow that had just given birth to some little pigs. Apparently the old sow did not understand Mr. Womble's intentions of reuniting her with the pigs, for she turned on him, pinning him to the ground. Never had such a struggle ensued between man and beast as it did that day, according to Mr. Womble. As a result of the onslaught he was so badly hurt that he could barely make it back to the house. But even in the midst of his wife's washing off blood and dirt from the wounds, he was so amused when she asked him, "Allen, pray tell, just what was you doing all the time that the hog was tearing you apart?"

Perhaps needless to say, Mr. Womble was a farmer in Grady County where he was born in 1907 and lived all of his life. His grandparents moved down to Grady County from north Georgia. He learned self-reliance from the circumstances of his life, one of which was the death of his father when Allen was only eleven years old. He worked at intervals during his life at such jobs as buying and selling scrap metal and fishing commercially at Shell Point. And always, of course, there has been his farming. His wife maintains that he has also always had an exceptional mechanical ability, and that whenever the need arose he could make a car out of almost nothing.

When it was suggested that Mr. Womble tell a story, his family immediately laughed and said, "He'll keep you sitting here all night he knows so many tales." And while the tale is in progress, nothing else exists for him at the moment. Nothing hurries him, for the stories are told slowly, with much detail. Even when Mrs. Womble says, "Allen, they don't want to hear all that part about what you thought at the moment," he tells her, "You want me to hit just the high places and miss all what makes a story good." So one settles back for a hair-raising witch tale or a humorous account of a coon-monkey (see tale 42) and realizes, along with his wife, that truly "tale-telling must have been born in him."

M. P. Maxwell

The rather drab setting of his housing-project home strangely belied the lively, humorous little man who lived within it in 1972. The man was M. P. Maxwell, who lived in Grady County except for seven years when he lived in Arkansas. He later resided at Glenmore Nursing Home near Thomasville.

Mr. Maxwell's immediate response to my appeal in the *Cairo Messenger* for assistance in gathering folktales in 1972 is indicative of his response seemingly to most things in his life. Whether he was talking of local history or present-day happenings in Grady County, there was an enthusiasm which showed in his entire face.

He believed that, by and large, the rural people in the county have been overlooked most of the time, except when politicians or salesmen wanted something from them. "It is out in the country where people struggled," he maintains, "and their story should be told." Mr. Maxwell believed that when people have to struggle so hard even to survive, then their stories of heroism should be preserved for posterity.

Mr. Maxwell chose to write his stories down rather than tell them, for he said that he needed time to organize his thoughts in telling certain incidents. And write them down he did. Every few days there would be a letter waiting for me in my mailbox with not only stories but also historical accounts of Grady County.

Many of Mr. Maxwell's stories are examples of the tall tale or the lying tale, but others are personal reminiscences involving incidents of local people in the county, such as the day his friend got caught chewing tobacco in school. He has contributed much valuable information that could ultimately be used in presenting a more historical record of the county.

Leroy Mann

Mr. Leroy Mann was a good example of what he prescribed for a good life, that "each man must have confidence in himself." For at eighty-one, Mr. Mann's whole bearing denoted a healthy self-confidence, whether he was talking about his past or his then-present life. He died in Grady County in 1977.

Mr. Mann learned early about self-reliance, becoming, for example, an excellent machinist through experimentation and experience. His father was a machinist, working with cotton gins. Each day when he was seven years old, Mr. Mann carried his father's lunch to him in his little red coaster wagon. And each day after dinner he would carry around his father's tools in his wagon and experiment with them. Thus, when he was thirteen years old and his father was injured at the cotton gin, he was able to step right into his father's position as a machinist.

In making a living for his large family, Mr. Mann ran the gamut of different occupations—hauling blocks; setting up and running all kinds of machinery, especially cotton gin equipment; farming all kinds of land and raising a variety of crops such as cabbage and sugarcane; running a restaurant; and building and running his own store.

But in all of his jobs Mr. Mann was pretty much his own boss, handling each task in his own way. Through his experiences he emerged a very self-contained man. There were many happy experiences in his life, but there were also some deeply tragic times. He recalled the time that, with his first wife (to whom he was married for over sixty-two years), he lost two daughters, a mother, and his best mule within a four-month period.

When asked how he came to have had so many experiences and to know so many trades, he said in 1972: "When you've lived to be eighty-one years old, you've been through many good and bad times, and you've learned a lot on your own because you had to."

Introduction

Allie Ben Prince

At seventy-two years old (at the time of the interview in 1972), Mr. Allie Ben Prince swore that he had never had more than one aspirin in his life. Such a statement could well be believed when one met Mr. Prince, for he seemed as stalwart and healthy as most men of forty. He said that his secret for continued good health was "hard work and frolicking"; his youthfulness might well be attributed to a genuine love of life.

He took great pride in his work, whether it was farming or driving the school bus. But it is the latter that he talked about the most. For thirty-five years he drove buses for the schools in Grady County. In some families he had "hauled" two generations of children to and from school. When he first began driving the bus, he used an old Model-T Ford, which really tested the capabilities of the driver. Often on bad roads he had to hold the gear in place to keep it from jumping out. If it did jump out, then he would lose his brakes. Those very early buses were quite crude compared to the plush models of today. On each side of the bus's interior were two wide planks with sawdust or cotton on them, and over that was placed a type of oil cloth. In the days when he made two rounds, he had to leave about four o'clock in the morning and return about sunset every night.

Even though he frequently carried as many as 110 children at one time, he said with pride that he maintained discipline on his bus and that parents would feel safe in having their children ride with him. His method of discipline was simple but effective. First, he respected and loved the children. Second, he made them know that he meant what he said.

But a man needs play as well as work, Mr. Prince believed. He laughed about his younger days when he worked from sunup to sundown, came in, took a bath in a tin tub (having no bathtubs back then, he would draw a tub of water and let it stand in the sun all day to warm it), walked several miles to a square dance, stayed until about one o'clock, walked home, changed back into his work clothes, and plowed the mules at sunrise.

When he was not going to a square dance, he was going to a fox hunt. For fox hunting was one of his great loves in life. Even at the time of his interview, he took great pride in his hounds and recalled the names of those from years ago that were excellent dogs, such as Dan Pipper, one that he got from Kentucky. Sometimes when he and his wife were younger, Gladys Prince would go with him on the fox hunts. They would take along some corn-flakes and milk, so if things got slow they could sit in the truck or wagon and eat cereal and talk.

Thus, Mr. Prince was a very warm and very genuine man. To Grady County residents, Mr. Prince was known as the longest reigning Santa Claus. For at least fifty years, he sported the red and white suit at Christmas. In his experiences as Santa he brought much laughter and sometimes a few tears. The tears frequently erupted when a frightened child looked skeptically at the jolly man with the long, white beard. Mr. Prince's Christmastime occupation had some very sad moments, too. He said that once while playing Santa to an extremely poor family in Whigham—there were eight children—Santa himself almost cried.

All in all, Mr. Prince had qualities that made him admirable not only to Grady Countians, but to people everywhere. He died in Grady County at the age of seventy-eight.

Athelone Barrett

The only female storyteller I interviewed seemed to personify Edgar Lee Masters's Lucinda Matlock, the woman who admonished the younger generation to give more to life, reminding them that "it takes life to love life." Seventy-one at the time of the interview in 1976, Mrs. Barrett talked excitedly of going to the coast to dig oysters, of fishing for catfish with "golden grubs," of having long talks at the table with her children.

Cooking and good food are synonymous with Athelone Barrett, perhaps necessitated by her background of preparing meals for large families. She was one of fourteen children herself and has eight children of her own, plus twenty-two grandchildren and eight great-grandchildren. She said that she had run the gamut of stoves in her lifetime, beginning with the old woodstove. "I had a big range—with reservoir warming closets—and then I bought me a five-burner oil stove, and then I went to electric. Then quit my electric and went to gas. That gas can't be beat in cooking." Many is the time when she has fed thirty-five "hands" a day during tobacco season.

Farming has been a way of life for the Barretts, both of whom share a love for the independence that the rural life can bring. As she puts it, "You're your own boss. You can quit when you want to. That's the part we like about it." In the past, on their farm of over two hundred acres, they raised sugarcane and cotton. Later, they turned to other, less demanding crops. "Some nights," Mrs. Barrett said, "we didn't gather into the house to eat until nine o'clock, trying to weigh up cotton and get them [the hands—mostly black] all back to town."

A flair for storytelling seems to be inherited from her mother's side of the family, for she recalls hearing stories from her mother that had been told to her by her mother's father. In fact, her maternal grandfather, who was a full-blooded Irishman, passed down many of his stories. Mrs. Barrett has a heritage of ghost lore in her family, beginning, so she said, when her grandfather bought a house on the old stagecoach road between Bainbridge and Camilla on the Flint River. It was there that the stagecoach drivers changed horses. Many stories supposedly grew up around some murders which took place on that road. Mrs. Barrett explained: "Mama said that back then they figured that the people traveling with stagecoaches had a lot of money. They would murder them and just pitch them over in the Flint River to get them out of the way, and they never knowed what become of them."

The house where the Barretts have lived now for about thirty-five years was itself haunted once by a ghost, but they removed the partition which had created a bedroom, and the ghost left. When the ghost appeared, it was always in that room. Three people were visited by the ghost, which Mrs. Barrett described in the following manner: "It doesn't have a head. It just looks like a woman in a white nightgown." But Mrs. Barrett always maintains that these are true stories. Whatever the case, they are certainly real to the Barrett family where they will probably continue to be perpetuated for generations to come.

Introduction

Elmer Wilcox

The visit with Elmer and Ossie Lou Wilcox produced, along with some delightful folktales on preachers and Irishmen, some historical anecdotes, local folk beliefs, and burial practices of the past. As Grady County coroner for over two decades and as an employee at Clark's Funeral Home in Cairo, Mr. Wilcox has mingled with all classes of people under all kinds of circumstances.

He was born on August 4, 1914, one of eight children. Ossie Lou, his wife, said that "back then they really had time to talk," and Mr. Wilcox recalled pre-television days where the family "would sit around the fire and shell peanuts and flip them hulls in the fire." He diagnoses what is wrong with families today: "There's not any communication—nothing; they don't even see each other."

Mrs. Wilcox said that she remembered hearing Elmer's sister tell about playing the game of "preaching" where they took "opening the doors" of the church literally.

> One thing that one sister said has stayed with me. She said that when their parents would go to town, that's when they had their big time. She said she can remember in the summertime they would have preaching (they didn't call it church; they'd have preaching), and one brother would preach; he really is a minister now. But he would preach; they'd close all the windows and the doors—and it would be so hot—and then he'd preach, and they'd sing and carry on. Then they'd open the doors of the church at which time they'd open the windows and doors.

Another sister, she remembered, said that the Wilcox family had its own definition of what the awkward age of children is. "It was when you were too little to get to go to town with your parents [alluding to an older tradition in the county of going to town only on Saturday], but you were too big to have something brought home to you."

Mr. Wilcox apparently admired much about his grandfather, specifically his staunch beliefs and his occasional pranks. In spite of his later blindness, his grandfather retained an excellent sense of humor. His devotion to the Baptist church took priority in his life even above his work. Mr. Wilcox recalled, "I don't care what work they had or what had to be done, Saturday at eleven o'clock he was at that church conference. . . . Everything was set aside. He used to grow about a hundred acres of sugarcane, and in the fall of the year that mill was shut down for that church service." It was from his grandfather that Mr. Wilcox learned many stories. He told of a trick that his grandfather played on a Watkins salesman, who was making it a regular practice to spend the night at his grandfather's house.

> Yeah, he used to tell me an old tale about this old—what were they?—Raleigh salesmen or Watkins salesmen, or something. They'd have an old covered wagon, and they'd come around peddling little spices and flavors. Granddaddy said he—the salesmen—would want to spend the night with him every week or month, however often he come there. And Granddaddy had a big lot there and a lot of extra stables; he said he had to feed his horse. So he went down there and rubbed his-self down with some sulfur or asafetida. Then he came back and made out like he was clawing or scratching his-self. He said way in the night he missed that fellow—he'd done got up and hitched up his mules and left. And he said he never did spend another night with him. He thought that Granddaddy had that seven-year itch that was going around.

Mrs. Wilcox added a footnote to the story, explaining that sulfur was a big medicine for the seven-year itch. And as for asafetida, she remembered seeing black children with little bags of it worn around the neck to ward off germs.

In Mr. Wilcox's work with the funeral home and in his position as coroner, he is very aware of the changes that have come in burial practices over the years. He explained, "Of course, they didn't have the funeral parlors—the body went back to the home. The neighborhood had to look after things for you, to take care of them. But now the modern funeral director just about takes the load off you. But, of course, there's still a few of the old people that want, maybe, to take them back home."

Most of the tales told by him are about preachers or the church. He was raised a Baptist but later married into Methodism. All of his tales are humorous ones, perhaps providing a needed change from the many grim duties he has to perform.

The Tales

Tales of the Dead

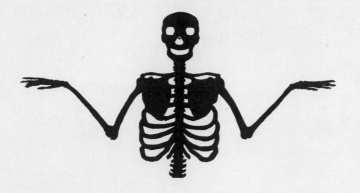

In 1946 Stith Thompson wrote: "Almost universal, except among the most sophisticated groups, is the fear of the dead" (*The Folktale*, p. 40). The world of the dead may be indeed for Hamlet the "undiscovered country from whose bourn no traveller returns," but in folktales such is not the case. For even in Grady County tales the dead supposedly do return, and if they do not visibly return, many a story is built around the fear that they will do so. The ghosts in the tales collected here do not seem to be terribly vindictive but seem instead to delight in lurking around derelict buildings to frighten travelers.

Frequently, the tales involve traveling people. For even after the coming of the automobile, people in rural areas usually could not afford a car and had to rely upon the horse and buggy or mules and a wagon. So if there was traveling at all, it was very slow and cumbersome. As no overnight accommodations were available in the county, the traveler was maintained through the hospitality of residents. If there happened to be a room available in the home, the traveler was usually invited to spend the night and share meals. If there should be no room, apparently the traveler would be directed to a deserted house where he might at least have shelter over his head. In any event, many stories grew up around travelers seeking shelter in old abandoned houses or churches.

1 · Racing a Ghost

This happened years ago in the old horse-and-buggy days. They didn't have motels and hotels as they do now, and this traveling salesman was going through the country driving a horse and buggy and selling his goods. He had to have a place to spend the night that night. The sun was sinking real low in the west, and he decided he better look for him a place. He came by this beautiful white house in the country, and, well, there was nobody living there. He couldn't understand it, but he drove on down the road about a half a mile, and he came to this little bitty house. People were living in there, so he stopped and asked the people if he could spend the night. The lady told him, "No, we just don't have room here in this house; it's rather small."

And he said, "Well now, tell me this. I passed a large house back up the road about a half a mile. Does anyone live there?"

She said, "No, no one lives there. It belongs to us."

He said, "Well, why couldn't I go up there and spend the night in that house?"

She said, "Well, Mister, it would be fine; but you know something, ghosts is around that house up there. Everybody calls it the hainted house."

He said, "Oh, I don't believe in ghosts; there's nothing to it."

She said, "Well now, I'm just telling you like it is. Now, if you want to try it, we'll spare you a blanket here, and we'll give you one of these kerosene lamps to keep light. They got a good fireplace, and there's wood in the old house; you can build you a fire if you want to."

Well, he thanked her very much, and he turned his horse around and rode back up the road and stopped at this house that nobody lived in. And he took his horse out, fed him, and put him in the lot, and he went on in the house. It was just about dusk dark, so he built him a little bitty fire in the fireplace; he had some sandwiches that he carried along for places like this, and he ate a sandwich. It was summertime, and the night was hot, so he had the door open. And all at once he noticed a big black cat walked in the front door, and he sat down over there by the fireplace. "Well," he thought, "maybe it's an old cat that stays here." The old cat sort of meowed around over there a little bit, and, well, it didn't sound exactly right to him; but he just accepted it as being a cat. So he settled in a little while, and the fire in the fireplace dwindled down, and he just got sleepy. He decided then he'd light the kerosene lamp and put it close to his bed, and he'd go to sleep. So he lit the lamp, and he turned it down low, and he took the blanket down there that the lady gave him. There was an old bedstead left in there that they didn't need, and he decided to sleep on it.

Lying down on the old bedsprings and the blanket, he got kind of comfortable, and he had just started to doze off to sleep. All of a sudden, though, he felt some cold hands coming up over his neck. Well, he lay there and didn't say a word, and shivers just ran up and down his spine; and he opened his eyes and looked, but he didn't see anything. So he said, "Oh, that's my imagination." He turned over on his other side and began to doze off, and he'd gone almost to sleep; then he felt those cold hands coming up around his neck again. He lay there, and he was so afraid he couldn't even speak; he couldn't holler. After a while, he heard a voice saying, "There ain't nobody here but me and you." He didn't say anything, but the voice repeated, "There ain't nobody here but me and you."

He said, "No, if you'll wait till I get on my pants, there won't be anybody here but you!"

So he jumped up out of that bed, and he jumped in his pants, and he didn't take time to even get his horse out. He just ran out of that door—he was after getting away from that house. He ran down the road about a half a mile; and he thought that he had left whatever it was at the house. All of a sudden, something patted him on the shoulder and said, "Buddy, can't we run?"

And he said, "Oh, my Lord, you haven't seen no running yet!"

So he tore out again down the road, and after a while something patted him on the shoulder and said, "Buddy, can't we run though?" So the man, he tore out again, and you know the last time I heard of this man, this salesman, they were both going down the road. Of course I couldn't hang around, because I had on paper clothes, and I was afraid the wind might blow or it might rain. So, I suppose that he's running yet.

2 · Ghost of a Baby

A long time ago in this part of the country, in south Georgia, people would, in the fall of the year, get a covered wagon. Two men, maybe three, would get the best mules that they had to a wagon, and they would take off to the coast. Carry their feed along and all, you know, and it'd take about three days to make the trip. That was before it was settled, but just by a little bit.

Two of the men going on this trip got way down there at the edge of Florida, and time come when it was dark and they wanted to spend the night. They passed a house, and it didn't look like nobody lived in it, so they didn't know if it would be all right; they just journeyed on.

When they got down to this next house, which was about three quarters of a mile, they stopped. And they asked the man who lived there, "My friend, this house back up the road there, does anybody live there?"

He answered, "No, there isn't nobody lives there."

He said, "Well, what we wanted to know is, it looks like it might come up some bad weather, and we would like to have shelter for our mules and have a place to spend the night."

"Well, they ain't nobody lives there, and there ain't nobody cares if you want to spend the night, for that matter; but you can't spend the night there."

He said, "Yeah, I mean if they don't nobody care, we'll just go back on up and spend the night."

"No, I don't think you could do it," he said. "That place, well, ain't nobody been able to spend the night in there in a long time."

The traveler said, "Now, if you don't care, we'll go spend the night there."

"Well, okay," the other man said. "But in case y'all change your mind now, you can stay here with me and my wife. We don't have but the one bed, but you could sleep on a pallet or somewhere."

"No, we've got our own bedding. We'll just go back up there. We don't want to put you out or anything."

"Well, okay, okay, go ahead. But in case you decide not to spend the night there, come on back down here and we'll lay pallets or put your bedding here."

"Well, if we decide to, we will."

So the two travelers went back up there. They drove up in the yard and unhitched the mules and went and put 'em in the little old log crib, a shed with a cow stall on one side and a mule stable on the other—you know, where the people had lived there, had about ten or twenty acres cleared up to make a living off of. When they went in, lo and behold, there the bedding was, what was left of it, and the old cook stove and everything—the furniture still in the house, tables and what have you. One of them said, "Well, what you want to do? Get some wood and build a fire?"

The other said, "No, you better not put fire in the stove there. We don't know what shape the pipe and all is in. We might burn the house down, or something."

"Well, I'll tell you. Let's just get us some wood and we'll just cook here on the fireplace."

"Well, all right then, we'll do that." So he went in the kitchen which was right in the little shed room, you know—the dining room and the kitchen was just in there—and got him a bench, and they built them a fire in front of the old stick and dirt chimney. One set on one end of the bench and one on the other, with their legs crossed. And they had cooked their beans and potatoes and was setting there by the fire talking about the rest of the trip on down; directly, one of the fellows says, "Hey, have you noticed anything?"

The other fellow said, "Hum, you mean that cat there in the corner, there by the fire? Yes, I saw him there."

"Well, did you see him when he went there?"

"No," his friend answered. "The first time I seen him, he was setting right where he's setting now."

"Well, now I don't exactly like cats. If it's all right with you, I'll send him on his way."

"Go ahead." So he reached over and got one of his boots, and he threw it at the cat. They didn't see the cat move, but the cat was setting on the other side of the hearth, still in its same position. Well, he didn't know if he had missed the cat or what had happened. But, anyhow, he reached down and got his other boot and that time really let it drive right where that cat was. They didn't see no cat move, but it was back in its first place.

He said, "Well now, that is a pretty fast cat, but I think I can stop it." So he reached in his back pocket and he pulled out his .38 and he shot the cat. They didn't see him move, but he was on the other side. So the man just emptied his six-gun, back and to, back and to; and the cat was still there. Then the cat just went away. And the man said, "Well, that done it for the cat."

They was setting there eyeing each other then, and they heard this little noise back in the kitchen.

One man said, "You hear that?"

"Yeah, I heard it," the other said.

"What did it sound like to you?"

"Well, I couldn't quite make it out. It must have been a screech owl or something like that." But he said, "I'm not afraid."

"Well," the other said, "I'm not afraid, but if that owl will just go on, that'll suit me fine."

Directly, the guy that was setting on the end of the bench, facing the kitchen door, looked in at the door. They had decided before then to fasten the door, but it didn't have no fastener on it, so they just pushed it to, and it swung back open a little ways. The guy looked in the crack of the door, and his eyes popped. And the other guy that was with him, he just wrenched around, and they seen this thing a-standing in the door. It was a baby. And its little fingers was just a-hanging down, and there wasn't no meat on it. It was a skeleton, just standing there, looking. So they just vacated the house! And they left their team there.

They went on back down to the other house, and they woke the man up. Said, "My goodness, man, we can't stay up there."

He said, "I told you."

"Well, I'm not afraid," one of the travelers said, "but now that kinda got into me. What happened?"

"Well, it's a long story," he said. "Me and my wife, and this fellow and his wife, moved down here and homesteaded this forty acres apiece; and we built our houses. He become dissatisfied, and he wanted to go back, but he didn't right off. Either one or the other of us would go into town (which was a good long ways; I don't know how far, but it would take a couple of days) to go get the supplies."

One would go for these supplies, and the next time the other guy would go for the supplies at that time. You kind of swap and turn about.

He said one day his neighbor took off to get the groceries and stuff and didn't come back. He said the man's wife was in bad health all along, and he said, "I didn't know he was going, and my wife didn't know."

So he went ahead, and he said it was a couple of weeks before he caught up enough with the work to go up there for a visit to see about her—you know, there was so much work to do clearing the land, and plowing, and tending the ground and all. When they got there, they went in, and the woman had taken sick and died. And the little baby, about two years old, well, it was just left there on the mercy of the world. So there was a little flour in the barrel, and the baby would go to that flour can or keg or whatever, and it would eat that flour until there wasn't very much in it, see. When it finished the flour, it starved to death. So the house become hainted. The kid, see, he was out making his rounds with the flour on its little apron, just a stack of bones.

3 · Ghost Gives Pot of Gold

I reckon it's been quite a few years back—I just do remember this one, about the ghost tales. They said this old lady was poor—she didn't have anything—and she'd went from house to house trying to live with other people. And they got tired of her and just told her not to come back anymore. So this old house was there; the people had run off and left it furnished, because they saw ghosts there. Well, she went to this old house; they told her she could have it if she'd stay in it—it could be hers. She went there to that house, and she went in that night. She shut the door and went to cook her some supper, and while she was cooking supper, the front door opened, and the back door opened. So she went to shut them again and went back to her supper. And as she went to eat, this man walked in and set down at the table with her and told her he was hungry, too. And she said, "Well, I haven't been seeing you around here." And he decided, well, he'd tell her that he was a ghost. But he couldn't never make up his mind to tell her, so she got scared when he wouldn't answer her. And she run out the back door, and as she went to run out she said, "I'm not staying here with you anymore!"

"Oh yes, lady, you will. I'm here to be with you. But I don't want to harm you. I want to give you a good deed." So he said, "Come on."

After she got out on the steps, she realized that people always said that if you saw a ghost, ask them what they wanted, and they'd tell you. So she turned around and came back in, and she said, "Just what do you want that you're coming up here bothering me for?"

He said, "Well, if you'll come and go with me, I'll show you want I want." And she followed him out in the yard to a big tree, and he said, "Dig." She dug down and found a pot of gold. So her neighbors envied her and wondered why she lived so good ever afterwards.

4 · The Ghost of Rit Hayes's Wife

Well now, this came from my mama and daddy. They knew Mr. Rit Hayes well. He didn't live very far from where my daddy lived. And everybody knew that Mr. Rit Hayes could see ghosts, or he said he could. Well, there was different things told on him, but my daddy said this happened on a Saturday night— he said very seldom would Mr. Hayes be caught off after dark; he just wouldn't.

This time, though, he rode on horseback up to Pelham, Georgia—at that time Pelham was a small place. Something happened to detain him, and it was after nightfall. Papa said they heard a horse coming down the road just as hard as that horse could run. So, Papa's mama—that was Grandma Glenn—said, "Gus, you and Jerry better go outside; I know who that is coming, and more than likely he's gonna stop here: that's Mr. Hayes. And if he does, y'all take the horse and go on and put him in the lot." Sure 'nuff, that horse got right in front of the gate; Mr. Hayes said, "Whoa!" pulled back and stopped that horse so quick. Mr. Hayes just threw them the bridle reins, and he ran right on in the house. Papa said him and his brother put the horse in the lot, and they came in, and Mr. Hayes told them there was a woman riding back of the saddle with him. Now, Mr. Rit Hayes's wife died several years before that, and he lived by himself; but he would see her on occasion. And she was riding in the saddle back of him. They said he wouldn't even go home that night. He spent the night there at the house.

That was just one of the episodes. Now, Mr. Hayes told different things. He told around in the country that some nights—he wouldn't see her every night, but only some nights—she would come and just stand up at the foot of his bed. One night he went out to the well to get some water. He woke up thirsty, and there wasn't any water in the house—of course, they had to go to the well and draw water. He went to the well and drew him up a bucket of cool water and said she was standing there at the well.

Now, he told the people around—different ones—the first time he saw anything, they had been to a big picnic. And, naturally, most of the time they carried dinners to a picnic, they'd have a bunch of dinner left over and they'd come in and bring it back that night. And he said they were out on the back porch eating what they had left over from the picnic. He said the prettiest little colt horse ran up out there in the yard and just neighed. He said that's the first thing that ever happened to make him think that his wife's ghost was visiting him.

Witch Tales

It is possible, Stith Thompson said, that ogres, giants, and even trolls at times may be of double natures, sometimes playing the cruel monster, sometimes the kindly helper. But not so witches: "Nothing but evil can be said for witches and their like" (*The Folktale,* p. 250).

When the Bible states, "Thou shalt not suffer a witch to live," it echoes the fear that people have always had concerning the destructive supernatural powers that may be attributed to a fellow human being or to some half-human creature (Exod. 22:18). If the fear of witchlike powers could be ascribed only to Matthew Hale days, then the fascination for witch tales might have ended in the seventeenth century. But witch tales still abide and continue to excite audiences.

Mr. Allen Womble in Grady County claimed to have met in his younger days, a very authentic witch who related some genuine witch tales to him. Mr. Womble's witches seem to exhibit most of the characteristics which Stith Thompson ascribes to these creatures, mostly females with long black hair: they turn into animals, especially bats, pigs, and horses; they parody religious services and delight in casting spells. And they love to steal children. Mr. Womble's storytelling witch was named Ila Gilly and lived around Bancroft, Georgia (between Bainbridge and Arlington), in the early part of this century.

5 · How to Become a Witch

The old gal (Ila Gilly) was really a witch and could ride you at night, believe it or not. Oh, yeah, and a witch can come to your house at night, put a spell on you, and—now this is far-fetched—she can turn you into a horse, a pretty white horse with a gold-braided saddle, and just get out and go. Now we'll get back to the tales she'd tell every night. Some of 'em I can remember, and some weren't too outstanding. It was in the wintertime, so we'd set around the fire and listen to these witch tales.

There was this girl who wanted to be a witch, so she got in with this other witch who was recruiting witches. The witch told her, "I'm going to make a witch out of you—just think of all the things you can do. If you want to throw an itching spell on somebody, or if you wanted to make them go into spasms or make the old man fuss at the wife or the wife fuss at the old man, you can make almost anything happen by saying the right words or calling on the evil spirits."

"Well," this girl said, "yes I do, I do want to be a witch."

The woman said, "I tell you what: we'll come by and pick you up Saturday night, and we'll ordain you into witchhood."

"But I can't leave the house."

"Why not?" the woman asked.

"My daddy and mama would skin me alive if I left the house; they'd be uneasy to death."

The woman said, "I'll fix it where they won't miss you until you're back. I'll come and knock on your window and put them fast asleep so they won't know you're gone."

So Saturday came. The woman called for the girl and told her that her parents were fast asleep and to come along with her. So they walked down the lane to the public road, but this was still not a paved road. The girl kept asking, "Where are we going?" But the woman said, "Don't you worry about it now."

About that time there came six pretty white horses, prettiest things you ever saw. Saddled and bridled. Oh, they were something nice. But there was two of them didn't have a rider. So the woman and the girl, they got on and rode and rode in the night. Pretty soon the girl didn't know where she was. This was so strange because she knew that country. But everything seemed so changed. It was pretty country; oh, it was so beautiful. They rode on and on, and directly they saw this big tower, all lighted up; it was so shining and bright. And there was some white horses there, so many of them, all saddled and bridled with gold braid around the saddles. So they got down and walked in on this huge, long stairway, all lighted up something terrible. They went in, and they were having a dance or ceremony of some kind. She told the girl, "Now, I'm going to make you a witch. You just repeat after me. Whatever I say, you say, and don't say nothing but what I say."

So this old witch with her long black hair draped over the back of her big fancy chair was just a-sitting up there, and around her throne was numbers of people. Well, the old witch asked if there was any people present who wanted to become a witch to please come forward. Some went forward to receive the old lady's blessings or to show the latest tricks. Anyhow, it fell the young girl's turn. She slowly came to the old witch who told the young girl to say whatever she said. She took this wand that had the big diamonds in it and waved it over the girl's head who was standing down below her. The witch said, "I give all between the top of my head and the bottom of my feet to the devil."

The girl said, "Now maybe I don't want to be a witch as bad as I thought I did." The other witches around her kept whispering, "Go, say it, say it, say it."

There was disturbance in the air, so she waved that wand back over the girl and said, "Everything between the top of my head and the bottom of my feet I give to the devil."

Again there was dead silence. But slowly the girl began to speak. "Everything, everything between the top of my head and the bottom of my feet I give, I give to—the LORD!" In the flash of a bolt of lightning, everything was gone and in total darkness. She looked around, and there was nobody there but her. So she said, "Now what am I going to do? I'm in a mess here." She began to walk around, and she found her way out this little door, which was the back side of some fellow's plantation in an old cotton house. She finally found a little wagon road which she followed, which finally led her to the farmhouse. She then knew where she was, so she found her way back home and climbed into the window. But she didn't want no more witch as long as she lived.

6 · Witch Rider

O h, yeah, she told us one more. I guess there was several more, if I could just think of them.

This little boy, he was getting weaker and weaker every day. And this witch was riding him, and she would keep a-riding and keep a-riding him. They took him to the doctor, and the doctor said, "There's nothing wrong with him, I can't find a thing, just fatigue. What does he do?"

"Well," his parents said, "he don't do anything but just stay around the house and all."

He was just about ten or twelve years old. So this other woman, who was a safe cracker [a retired witch], so to speak, a witcher, she saw that they was overdoing it with the little child. She went to the parents of the kid and said, "I can break that spell." She said, "I can do it. The witches is riding him."

They said, "Well, I don't believe in no such thing, but if you can do it, I wished you would."

She said, "Well now, I can do it, but under this circumstance: I'll have to sleep with that kid."

"Well now, I don't know too much about that! But if that's all it takes, well, just go ahead."

So, the witch who was riding him would come in and make a creepy noise like a bat, see. The child would go into its trance, and then she would take him out and turn him into a pony, or whatever, and just go anywhere she wanted to go. She would bring him back in and make a screechy noise, and he'd go back in and go back to bed.

This witcher, or ex-witch—she'd probably been kicked out for naughty doings—she went to sleep with the kid. And she knew the noise, see. And when she made this little noise, "Lickty-skip and here we go," they would go. But when she made that little squeaky noise—anybody could say that—then you could turn the tables. So this witcher was laying in bed with the kid, awake, and she heard the squeaky noise and said, "Lickty-skip and here we go." She just took the little boy, and they got out there and they made a horse out of *her!* They rode that horse *all* night long until after sunup, and then took her to the blacksmith shop and had her shod. They knew her, so they took her home, and there the old man was.

Oh, he was out of his mind. "My wife is gone. She's been gone all night, I reckon. I don't know where in the world she could be. I just don't know where she could be." The witcher, the gal that could break the witchcraft on them, said, "You want to know where your wife is?"

"Well, I certainly do; I mean, I've been uneasy to death about her."

She said, "There she stands."

"Well, that's a horse!"

"Well, that's your wife."

"Oh, come on," he said, "I ain't in no mood for foolishness. I want to know where my wife is."

The witcher said, "Okay, I'll tell you what you do. You take the hammer and knock them shoes off the feet, turn her in the stable, and turn around three times. But be sure you lock the stable door."

He said, "Now, I'll knock the shoes off the horse if you say so, but I don't know what you're driving at."

She said, "Well, you do that. Then I'll tell you where your wife's at."

So he knocked the shoes off the horse and led her in the stable and pulled the bridle and saddle off her, or either just turned her loose, I don't know; but anyhow, he turned around three times and said, "Okay, now where's my wife?" She said, "She's in the stable." He looked into the stable and his wife was standing in there. She'd done turned back into his wife.

7 · Witch as a Hog

Another one Ila Gilly told me: She said this lady was going along the road, a back road. It was very thinly settled way back then during the time she was telling the tales; there wasn't too many people. She was going down the settlement road, the back road through the timber and all. And there was a man. He was out in the timber and he kept watching, watching. She saw him and kind of perkened up [perked up] her gait a little bit. And then, just to make sure if he was following her or not, she turned around and saw him again. He was still in the timber, but he was coming on up behind. So she really got to marching it off then; you know, she was getting gone. He just kept walking faster, too. But as luck would have it, there was two neighbor men that was sitting there by the side of the road. They had just met up and was set down for a conversation, and she just walked right up on them. She said, "Well, don't look now, but there's a man following me."

They said, "Well, who is it?"

She said, "I don't know, but he's right out there in the trees." He was coming on up, and they raised up and there the man was. So they just proceeded and said, "Now, we'll work you over, buster!" They was gonna catch him, so they took off after him. And he run and jumped behind a big pine, and they run on up there. They had him cornered right behind that big tree. "Oh, we got you now!" And there was a pig come out from behind the tree!

Numskull or Noodle Tales

The third and last major division in Aarne and Thompson's *Types of the Folktale* is the broad category "Jokes and Anecdotes." Leading the subdivisions under this category are the "Numskull Stories." These numskull or noodle tales are still popular in the Grady County area, with some narrators possessing small repertoires of the tales and others at least acknowledging that such tales were told by their ancestors.

Jan Brunvand in *The Study of American Folklore* defines the numskull and summarizes the various names ascribed to him: "'Numskull stories,' also called 'noodle tales,' attribute absurd ignorance to people, often to a particular group. In Denmark, for example, the traditional fools are the *Molbos*; in England they are the "Wise Men of Gotham"; and in the United States they may be two stupid Irishmen named 'Pat and Mike.'"[1]

In discussing the forms that the noodle's absurd ignorance may take, both Stith Thompson and William A. Clouston suggest numerous possibilities. In his synopsis on "Fools and Numskulls," Thompson itemizes several types of absurdities: mistaken identity, inappropriate and absurd actions, misunderstanding of the nature of animals, and an overlooking of elementary natural laws.[2] Thompson concludes, however, that "any logical arrangement of the activities of numskulls continually breaks down, since their absurdity is not confined to sensible bounds. One can only say that some fools are primarily ignorant and some primarily absent-minded" (p. 192). Clouston, in his definitive work on the numskull, seeks to delineate more specifically the characteristics of the noodle: thinking he is doing the clever thing, he follows

1. Jan Harold Brunvand, *The Study of American Folklore* (New York: W. W. Norton and Co., 1968), p. 110.
2. Stith Thompson, *The Folktale* (New York: Dryden Press, 1946), pp. 190–92.

instructions too literally; he is generally very honest in his good intentions; he entertains but one thought at the time and holds to it tenaciously; through his blunders he occasionally stumbles into good fortune. "In brief, he is—in stories at least—a standing illustration of the 'vanity of human life.'"[3]

Most scholars agree that it is difficult, if not almost impossible, to locate a tale's origin or source. Yet with the noodle tales' being part of the jestbook tradition, approximate dates can be assigned to those found, according to Clouston, "in the early Buddhist books, especially in the *Jātakas*, or Birth-stories, which are said to have been related to his disciples by Gautama, the Illustrious founder of Buddhism" (p. vii). Clouston, however, qualifies his conclusions by suggesting that the tales were current perhaps among the Hindus and date back a century prior to the Christian era. Thompson discusses the wide jestbook tradition, noting that many tales were later included in books of exempla in the Middle Ages but that they were nearly "always constructed on some ancient pattern" (p. 196).

Whatever the heritage of the noodle tales, remnants of the tradition survive in the southwest Georgia area in the form of Pat and Mike, two notorious, blundering, Irish numskulls. Alice M. Bacon, who placed the tales within the black tradition,[4] wrote in the *Southern Workman* in 1899:

> The antipathy of the Irishman to the Negro is proverbial, but perhaps it is not as well known to most of us that the Irishman has a place of his own in Negro folk-lore. Among the popular tales of every race may be found many dealing with the foolish performance of some one or more simpletons. . . . Sometimes he [the

3. William A. Clouston, *The Book of Noodles* (London: Elliot Stock, 1888), pp. x–xi.

4. Elsie Clews Parsons in her article "Folk-lore from Elizabeth City, Virginia" (1922), alluded to some of the material recorded in the *Southern Workman*. She wrote, "The most notable part of Miss Bacon's collection is, I think, the so-called 'Irishman Stories.' These noodle tales have a wide distribution in the South; and Miss Bacon was the first recorder, as far as I know, to recognize the place of the tales in the hospitable folk-lore of Negroes" (*JAF* 35 [1928]: 251).

numskull] is merely a member of an alien race who makes himself foolish by his lack of knowledge of the ways of the country in which he is sojourning. Into this latter class must come the performance of the Irishman of the Negro story. It is generally safe when a story of any absolutely stupid performance on the part of anyone comes to you from a Negro, to set it down as an Irishman story, for the Irishman is the scapegoat upon whose head are piled all of the follies that ever man committed, and many that he never thought of committing.[5]

Clouston attributes the use of Irishmen to another cause: "The propensity with which Irishmen are credited of making ludicrous bulls is said to have its origin, not from any lack of intelligence, but rather in the fancy of that lively race, which often does not wait for expression until the ideas have taken proper verbal form. Be this as it may, a considerable portion of the bulls popularly ascribed to Irishmen are certainly 'old as the jests of Hierokles,' and are, more over, current throughout Europe" (p. 12).

8 · The Ass's Egg

There was this Irishman who had just come over to America and wanted a horse. Somebody sold him a pumpkin to hatch himself one. He stumbled by a tree up near where his pumpkin lay and up jumped a rabbit. He took off after the rabbit, and, seeing his long ears, he decided that he'd gotten a mule's papa instead of his horse.

9 · Hanging for Water

Now, Pat and Mike, they were walking one night, and they were very, very thirsty. And they were walking on the railroad, and it came to a stream; but the railroad was pretty high

5. "Our Duty to Dependent Races," *Southern Workman* 28 (1899): 192.

above the stream. And they were so thirsty; so Mike said, "Pat, I'd like to have a drink of that water."

Pat said, "Well so would I, but how we gonna get it?"

"Well I tell you, I'll hang down from this trestle here by my feet, and you climb down me, and I'll hold to your feet, and that will put you where your head then will reach the water. Then, I'll pull you back up, and then you let me down; and I'll get a drink of water."

Well, that sounded like a pretty good idea. So Mike, he held by his feet to the railroad ties, and Pat, he climbed down on him, and Mike got him by his feet. Well, he couldn't hardly hold him; he just couldn't, and his hands began to slip. He said, "Pat, hold on just a little bit; let me spit on my hands, they're slipping." So he turned a-loose to spit in his hands, so they wouldn't slip; and Pat got all the water he wanted that night.

10 · Mistaken Identity

Let me tell you about these two Irishmen in this town one time. Of course, this happened years ago. They were in this town, and they were coming, meeting one another down the street. And they decided they knew one another, but when they got a little closer, then they decided perhaps they didn't know one another. So, this is what one of them said when they met right close up: "Well, Pat, I saw you coming down the street. I smiled and you smiled. And you thought it was me, and I thought it was you; and it wasn't either one of us."

11 · Carrying Part of the Load

One day Mike went to get some corn ground into meal. But on the way home he got to worrying about the heavy load that his poor old horse was having to carry. So he said to his horse, "Well, now, never let it be said that I was cruel to my faithful old friend. I'll just unstrap the meal off your back and put it on my own, so you'll have me to carry, not the meal, too." And with that Mike rode happily down the road.

12 · Mule Wants to Ride

This man was riding horseback, and he was an Irishman, too. It was hot weather, so there was plenty of horseflies and yellow flies down around the creeks and branches. And he was riding down the road—went through this creek down there— and the horse kept kicking at the horseflies, shaking his head, trying to knock them off. After a while, the old horse kicked his two hind feet, and he got one of them caught in the stirrup of the saddle. And the old Irishman looked down at him and saw his foot in the stirrup. He said, 'Well, if you're gonna get up, I'll get down."

So, he hopped down off of him.

13 · Outrunning the Train

The only one I remember right now is about the Irishman who was going down the railroad tracks when a train came; they said he just run till he gave out. And the train came to a stop, and the engineer got out and said, "Why in the hell didn't you take to the bushes?" The man said, "Hell, if I can't outrun it here in the open, I know damn well I couldn't out in the bushes!"

14 · Green Persimmons

Well, this happened years ago to two Irishmen. I don't remember their names, but we'll call them Pat and Mike. They came over to this country, and naturally they didn't have any job and nowhere to go or eat. They were traveling down the road, and they didn't know anything about persimmons; and they saw this tree of wild persimmons right next to the road. Now, this was in the fall of the year, and persimmons were just beginning to turn red, but they wadn't ripe. Mike said, "Pat, look at that fruit. Isn't that beautiful?"

Pat said, "Yes, Mike, you reckon it's fitting to eat?"

Mike said, "Well, I don't know, but I'm mighty hungry; let's try it. Pat, you climb up the tree, and you shake them down; and we'll see if they're good to eat."

So Pat, he climbed up the tree, and he reached over—he decided he'd taste one of them—and he got him one of those green persimmons. Now, if you've ever tasted a green persimmon, you know what it will do to you. It will draw your mouth up just like you're fixing to whistle. So Pat, he bit down on that green persimmon; and Mike was on the ground watching him. And it drew Pat's mouth up just like he was fixing to whistle. Mike looked up and saw him and said, "Pat, what you whistling about? I don't hear nothing, but your mouth look like you fixing to whistle."

Pat said, "Mike, I ain't whistling, I'se poisoned! These things are poisoned!"

He jumped down out of the persimmon tree, and they went on down the road.

15 · Crossing the Stream

Pat and Mike was crossing this creek on an old log, a tree that had blown down across the stream—and, of course, it was a log then. They wanted to walk that log and get on the other side. And right in the middle of the stream, there was another limb hanging down off of a green tree, right over the log where they'd have to catch it and bend it out of the way so they could walk the log. So Mike, he went ahead, and Pat said, "Now, you take the limb and bend it on out of the way, and then we can walk across the log." So Mike, he got ahold of the limb, and he pulled, and he pulled it way back. And just about the time Pat got right over the middle of the stream, Mike, he let go of the limb, and it swung back around and just knocked Pat right in the middle of the stream.

Pat got out of the water, and he said, "Mike, why did you do that?"

Mike said, "Well Pat, if I'd've held that thing, it would've killed you, wouldn't it?"

Tales of Courting
and Marriage

16 · The Blind Fiancée

Well, in this community, a widow woman lived. Of course, she had some children, and she needed a husband awfully bad; there was nobody to make a living and nobody to care for the children. Not too far away from there an old bachelor lived. She'd been making eyes at the old bachelor, and I think he kind of liked her. But the word got around that the widow woman's eyesight was just about gone—that she just couldn't see—and the bachelor, he had got ahold of it. She was a little bit scared of what he might think.

The old bachelor, he was coming over that Sunday afternoon; and she decided she better trick him just a little bit on the eyesight, 'cause really she was about half-blind—she couldn't see well at all. So she called one of the children there on the front porch and said, "Son, take this needle and go out yonder and stick it in the fence right on the left-hand side of the gatepost. Stick it up in the fence, now, and just leave it there." After a while, her bachelor friend came along; they were sitting out on the porch, and they talked, and they talked, and evening went by swiftly. Finally she decided it was about time that she would ask him to stay and eat supper with her. About that time, though, she thought it was a good time to find the needle; so she called one of her little boys and said, "I see a needle out there on that gatepost. No, it's to the left of the gatepost. Run out there and get that needle. I can see it so good from here." The little boy, he went out there and brought the needle and give it to her.

The bachelor friend, he said, "Well, her eyesight must be all right if she can see a needle that far."

So, she told one of the little girls to go in there and set the table. She was going to ask the bachelor friend to eat supper. The little girl went in and put supper on the table, and everything was ready. The couple went in the front door and went back to the kitchen, and right in the middle of the table, the little girl put a bowl of yellow butter. And so this widow woman, she walked up to the table, and she slapped that butter clear off the table. And it hit over there and just broke all to pieces. She said, "Scat off of the table! I can't keep the cats off the table."

So that ruined the whole trick, didn't it?

17 · Anybody, Lord

This old maid, she wanted to get married so bad that she decided to pray to the Lord to send her a husband. So one night she went out of the house into the woods—you know, back then the houses in the country were usually surrounded by woods—and she found her an old oak tree. So she began to pray for a husband. While she was praying, an old hoot owl lit on a limb just above her and cried, "Who-who-who-o-o?" The old maid said, "Anybody, Lord, just send me anybody."

18 · Good Grammar

Let me see now, this happened years ago. When young men was courting the girls, they rode horseback most of the time. And this girl and her family lived out in the country, and she had a suitor who was coming to call on her. But the girl's daddy, he was very talkative, and he didn't talk too plain, and didn't use correct grammar when he spoke; and she got after him about it. She said, "Daddy, my friend's coming over Sunday. Now, I want you to talk and use good grammar like you ought to; I'm thinking a whole lots of him there, and maybe he'll propose to me some of these days."

He said, "Well daughter, I'll try my best to and especially the next time he comes. When did you say he's coming?"

She said, "Well, he's coming Sunday afternoon."

So the old man said, "Well, I just got to do better than I did."

So time walked on, and it came Sunday afternoon, when here comes his daughter's suitor down the road on horseback. The girl said to the daddy, "Daddy, you go on out and meet him now." So he went on out the porch, out in the front yard, about the time the young man rode up.

He said, "Howdy there, Charlie! I thought I knewed you when I see'd you came roding down the road. Hitch your horse and got down. Came in and sot down. Sue'll be down just as soon as she knewed you come."

So that old man, he got it slightly mixed up, according to the way we think and talk, but he did the best he could anyway. Now, I don't know whether they got married or whether they didn't.

19 · The Girl Who Ate So Little

There was this woman who had a boyfriend. And this boyfriend took her out to eat one night. The woman decided that she would use her very best manners to show what a lady she really was. So when her plate was brought to her, she very carefully cut each of her peas with a knife and ate half a pea each time very slowly.

Well, the boyfriend thought to himself that he had never seen anyone eat so daintily. Everything was going fine, when all of a sudden the lights went out and stayed out for about five minutes. When they finally came back on, the boyfriend looked over at his girl, and, lo and behold, she was choked stiff. She had crammed in all the peas with her hands when the lights were off.

20 · How Big the Cook's Mouth

O nce there was a state senator who had come home between sessions for a weekend. He came downstairs to breakfast the next morning where the black cook was preparing breakfast and decided he'd have some fun with her. He said, "You know, Annie, we've been making some mighty interesting laws up there."

She said, "Sho 'nuff?"

He said, "Yeah, why just the other day we passed one that women with small mouths could have at least two husbands."

Annie puckered up her mouth like a rosebud and squeaked, "You don't say!"

The senator said, "But then we passed another law that said that women with large mouths might have as many as four husbands."

Annie opened her mouth till it looked like a canyon and bellowed out, "Well, I do declare!"

21 · Four Old Maids

T here was these four old maids living together. Well, all of their boyfriends were coming to see them on the same night. They talked about it beforehand and decided that they would let each other know the next day how many times the boyfriends kissed them by saying the word *morning* for each kiss.

So the next morning the first one to speak said, "Good morning."

The second one came in and said, "Good morning, fine morning, this morning."

Then the third one came in with a large smile and said, "Good morning, fine morning, this morning. If it's as fine a morning in the morning as it is this morning, it'll be a fine morning in the morning."

The fourth one came in and said, "Howdy, durn it."

Humorous Tales
of False Fright

22 · Goat in the Pulpit

This tale came from a truthful man, and his name was Mr.
Will Daniels. He lived in our place; I knew him personally.
He told this on himself and another man, and he said it really
happened. He told me he was working when he was a young boy;
of course, he was a rather old man when I was talking to him
then, when they lived on our place. But a lot of times the boys in
the country, they'd walk to town on Saturday night or walk to
church. These two boys, Mr. Daniels and the other man (I forgot
his name—we'll call him Mr. Johnson, but they weren't really
quite grown), they walked to town that evening late. And they
stayed in town until after dark, then had to walk home. Naturally, they hadn't been out much at night, and they were a little
bit scared to go home. But they knew the way well, and they
started walking home. Mr. Daniels said about halfway from town
to their houses, it just came up a big rainstorm, just about the
time they got halfway. And he said it just started pouring down
rain. Well, they didn't want to get wet, and they were looking for
a shelter; and pretty close to the road there was an old log church
that had been thrown away. They wadn't using it anymore, but it
still had a shelter over it, and the old benches was in there, and
the old pulpit was up there. So he said, "Let's go in that old
church."

The other said, "Alright."

They ran in the back of that church and it was dark, ooh, and
just a-pouring down rain. And they sat in the back part of the
church—they wadn't sitting up towards the pulpit. So, they got to
listening; it was raining hard, but they could still hear something
on the pulpit (plunkity, plunkity, plunkity), walking around on
the pulpit. Well, one of them says to the other, "What is that?"

The other one said, "I don't know, but I don't especially like it."

Whatever it was kept walking around on the pulpit. So Mr. Johnson said, "Will, let's leave this place."

Will said, "No, it's just pouring down rain outside. Let's stay, and we'll see what it is."

After a while, whatever it was on the platform up there got down off the platform, coming down the aisle right towards them. And he said they could see something white even though it was real dark inside. Now, Mr. Will Daniels, he was no coward. He was one of the bravest men I've ever known; I don't think he was afraid of anything. He said, "I never wanted to run so bad in all of my life. It just looked like my feet wouldn't stand, and my partner was the same way." But they just grouped together then and decided they'd wait to see what it was. It was coming down the aisle towards them, a little closer and a little closer, until it got right even with them. And Will asked me, "What do you reckon it was?"

I said, "I don't know."

He said, "It was an old billy goat that had ran up there out of the rain and was up there on the platform, walking around. That's what it was."

23 · Frightened by Frogs

This happened back in the old horse-and-buggy days. This salesman was traveling through the country driving a horse-to-a-buggy, and he was from up north; he'd never heard any frogs hollering, and he'd never seen any lightning bugs even. But he was down south—there wadn't many hotels down there, and out in the country there wadn't any—and it was the custom, if he could find a place to stay, to pay whoever it was lived in the house for the overnight lodging. So, it was getting just about dusk dark, and he came to this house and asked the people who lived in the house about spending the night there with them. They said, "Yes, we have an extra room; we can put you up for the night. But our water is real short in the well; you'll have to take your horse down to that little old pond about a quarter of a mile down the road that you passed and water your horse down there."

The salesman said, "Well, that's alright."

He unhitched the horse from the buggy and took the harness off, and it was getting pretty close to dark. He had to lead his horse on down the road to the pond where he could drink water. And as he got down there, it began to get dark; and he saw sparks of fire just a-flying all over the woods. Soon he began hearing big fellows over there in the water; one of them said, "Grooppity-backa, grooppity-backa, grooppity-backa."

And the other one said, "Whip-cut-em-en-slash-em, whip-cut-em-en-slash-em, whip-cut-em-en-slash-em."

And another one over there said, "Mod-der-ration, mod-der-ration, mod-der-ration."

He lit out back up to the house, didn't even take time to water his horse, and hitched his horse to the buggy. The man came out there and said, "Say, aren't you gonna spend the night here at this house?"

He said, "No sir, I just tell you, I've never heard anything like it in my life. I went on down there to water my horse, and I heard things in the water over there. One of them said, 'Knee-deep, knee-deep.' The other one said, 'Whip-cut-em-en-slash-em, whip-cut-em-en-slash-em.' And a great big old monster over there—I reckon if he'd got ahold of me, there wouldn't 've been a piece left of me. He said, 'Mod-der-ration, mod-der-ation.' I looked up and sparks of fire was flying all over the woods, and I said, 'I'm getting out of here!' Get up from here, horse! Get up from here!"

And he checked out.

24 · Thief Reformed by Frogs

This old farmer, he went to town on Saturday evening, and he didn't have any money. And standing around the stores there, he wanted a chew of tobacco so bad. He didn't have any money, so actually he stole him a little piece of tobacco from the store. Well, he got out of the store, and it was about sundown when he started from town on back home. He was a-chewing tobacco, and he was a-chewing tobacco. And he came across a little pond, and he heard something out there say, "Knee-deep, knee-deep, knee-deep."

And he heard something over a little further saying, "Plug-a-tobacco, plug-a-tobacco, plug-a-tobacco."

He took out the piece of tobacco and threw it over in the water and said, "Here! The whole world's got to know that I stole a plug of tobacco. How did you know it, out there?"

And he checked out and left the tobacco and all in that pond.

25 · The Open Grave

B ack in the twenties or the real early thirties, we lived in this little old town. It wasn't very big, you know, about three hundred people. I drove a team, a log team. There was a lot of other guys drove teams too, snaking logs and what have you. But me and this here Johnny Brown, we'd make a little more money by taking care of all the stock after we come in. You know, a day's work then was from sunup until sundown; you worked all day long. We'd have to work after nightfall tending to the stock and getting them squared away and everything. So this night we took an unusually long time to get it done. But we had this path; we'd come through the corner of the graveyard so we'd be nearer to the sawmill. We'd go from the mill to the house through the corner of the graveyard.

Well, the pulpit committee or somebody there—anyhow, the caretakers of the graveyard—decided to have fresh flowers all during the wintertime. So they would dig them this flower pit, or greenhouse, and then put a cover over it and have the toolshed on top of that. So they decided that they would just dig that thing eight foot deep, ten feet long, and eight feet wide. Then they'd have enough room to put all the flowers in. So me and Brown went to work that morning, and right after we went to work, the workers went to dig the pit in the cemetery. And they just chose the place where we went through the graveyard there in our path. Yeah, they chose our path.

Well, I got off about ten or fifteen minutes before Brown did, so I got my horses fed. And he was gonna feed part of the mules and the oxen. But he drug around, so I just hung my coat over my shoulder and my bucket under my arm, and I was coming home. To keep from littering up the graveyard, now, they would roll that dirt off and put it in a ditch down in the lower edge of the graveyard. They'd keep it real clean, just shovel it in a wheelbarrow and carry it off. So here I was coming along with my coat and bucket, not paying no attention to where I was going, and I fell in the hole.

Well, it didn't hurt me; I mean, it just kind of shook me up, falling eight foot. I landed on my hands and knees. I said, "What on earth is coming off here!" Well, I then remembered I'd heard a little something about them digging this greenhouse. So I made several attempts to climb, and I saw there just flat wasn't no use. I mean, you just can't climb a steep dirt bank eight foot high. And knowing, too, that Brown would come on pretty quick and that he could help me get out, I just backed over in the corner. It hadn't been dark long, and looking up and out of the hole you could see anybody. But you couldn't see anybody looking down and *in* the hole, because it was dark down there. I just walked over and set down on the far side, wondering how I was gonna get out of there. And before I knew it, here come Brown in the hole with me. I said to myself, "Well, now, you know, if I'd just told him, he could have helped me out of here. Now he's in as bad a shape as I am." But it was dark. He hadn't saw me, but I could see him. So he done the same thing that I did: he fell up on the wall and made several attempts to climb out but couldn't make it. But I wasn't afraid then. I could climb on his shoulders and get out and then drag him out, see. Or he could climb out and drag me out. So we had it made.

While Brown was making his attempt to get out, I said, "You can't get out of here." And, boy, I ought not to have done it. There was a hail of clay and sand and grass down in there on me. That joker dug into that bank and was out and gone before you could say, "Don't!" He was already scared, and when I said, "You can't get out of here"—right up the bank! Left me stranded in the hole.

26 · Ghost Scaring the Ghost

These two plantation owners didn't live but about three or four miles apart, and both of them had a large number of slaves. So the slaves got to going from one plantation to the other at nighttime, and the plantation owners, they noticed it. One of them saw the other one a few days after that, and he said, "Well, you know our slaves are going from one plantation to the other."

The other plantation owner said, "Yeah, I know it. I'm afraid they're plotting some kind of devilment. Maybe we ought to do something about it."

So, they decided then on a scheme to stop it. In between the two plantations, there was this gallows. Oh, it was about fifteen feet high; from the ground there was a platform, and then above that they had a big timber run out where they could hang people.

"I tell you what let's do," one plantation owner said; "let's meet there next Tuesday night, say at about eight o'clock. They generally start about that time going from one plantation to the other. And we'll get up on that gallows, and we'll just scare them so bad that they'd be scared to pass by there at any other time."

So it was agreed upon. And the next Tuesday came around— their meeting day. One of them, he came over at the specified time, and he waited for the other one. And the other one just didn't show up right then. He waited around, and after a while he heard the slaves coming down this little old road through the woods—had to pass right by the gallows. He said to himself, "Well, I reckon my friend just couldn't make it. I'll hop up on the platform there, on that gallows, and I'll give them a good scare right by myself."

He climbed up; he had to be in a hurry, because the slaves were getting too close. He climbed up on the gallows, and he wrapped a white sheet around him, and he was standing still. When the slaves got close enough, one of them said, "Great goodness! What's that yonder?"

Another one said, "I don't know; I don't like it! Right on top of that gallows!"

Another one of the slaves, said, "Look a yonder, there's two of them!"

So the man up top, he began to look around, and he looked down underneath him; and sure 'nuff there was something standing down there with a white sheet on. Well, he got so scared hisself; he didn't know that his partner had come and didn't have time to get up on the gallows—he just run down under it and wrapped the sheet around him. But the one on the upper level, he didn't know that his friend had ever got there. And when the slaves said, "There's two of them!" he jumped down off of that scaffold, and he went running towards the slaves, wanting company. Naturally, the slaves, they tore out running. So the man said, "Wait! Wait! It's me!"

One of the slaves said, "Lord, he says he'll have one a week!"

And the owner said, "No, no, wait! Wait, it's me!"

The other slave said, "No, he don't want one a week. He says he'll have two a week!"

And they went down that road a-flying, with the plantation owner right behind them. And the last time I saw them, they was still going down the road.

27 · Fork in the Skirt

Version A

This old lady, she was brave; she'd do anything and everything. It didn't matter, for she wadn't afraid of anything. So some of them bet her one night that she wouldn't go to the cemetery to stick a fork in the grave where they could know she'd been out there. She told them she would go and stick this fork down in the grave. So she went up there; she was an old lady, and

97

she wore these old-fashioned aprons. Well, when she kneeled down to stick the fork in the grave, she stuck it through her apron. When she went to get up, she couldn't stand. She tried a couple of times and said, "Well, the man in the grave's got me!" And she got so scared she died a natural death right there. They found her out there when they went to find the fork in the grave, and she'd had a heart attack. It scared her to death.

Version B

They used to build these little shelters over the graves in the cemetery, just little shelters—I know you've seen them. There's not many of them now, but I was thinking about it the other day. We were out here at Pisgah cemetery, and there's one in there that this man, Mr. Butler, keeps up, painted and everything— just a little shelter over this baby's grave. I don't think it was but about eighteen months old when it died, but he keeps that grave and that little shelter over that grave just as nice as a man would his house.

They said that Mr. Butler would try to scare these folks' boys from coming in late—sometimes they'd be out on them parties, you know. He got on top of this little house with a sheet and his foot slipped. He got the sheet hung, and he couldn't get loose. They said he fainted, and they had to go out there and get him. He tried to scare them, and he fainted trying to scare them 'cause he thought the ghost had got him. People were really afraid of people after they died back then.

Tales of
Church-Related Humor

Rural Grady County, like most counties in Georgia, still has the church as a central part of not only religious activities but social events as well. Its prominence was paramount especially throughout the early part of this century. A typical Baptist church might hold, in addition to the regular Sunday service(s), a weekly prayer meeting (usually Wednesday), revivals (protracted meetings) twice a year, class parties, and fifth-Sunday meetings (a joint meeting of several churches on the fifth Sunday of a month, lasting all day and including "eating on the grounds" and all-day preaching). A very accurate account of gatherings on special Sundays is given in A History of Georgia, edited by Kenneth Coleman and others: "Every mother then brought the best she could afford: fried chicken, ham, fish, biscuits, cornbread, vegetables, pies and cakes. People moved from table to table, sampling food from as many different families as possible and eating 'enough to help them plow for a week.'"[1]

The churches were usually centrally situated in the community, incorporating several acres of nearby land where the cemetery was located. The typical church building was quite open, having no screens on the doors and windows. It was, therefore, not unusual for birds, bats, dogs, or even a goat to seek sanctuary within the building, sometimes right in the middle of a sermon. William W. Rogers, a noted historian on neighboring Thomas County, gives an account of canine interference during a church service in Thomasville (less than fifteen miles from Cairo): "It was very annoying to preacher and congregation to have a cur bay the moon from the church door, or to indulge in sharp, ear-splitting barks from the aisles at the sexton, as he vainly endeav-

1. Kenneth Coleman et al., eds., A History of Georgia (Athens: University of Georgia Press, 1977), p. 335.

ors to induce him to retire in good order. . . . There were frequent reports of dogs snoring in church. One bold animal even took refuge in the pulpit while a sermon was in progress."[2]

Most rural churches in the southwest part of the state were either Baptist or Methodist, but whatever the denomination, the church wielded strict Calvinistic control over the moral lives of its members. Yvonne Brunton in her book *Grady County, Georgia*, recounted the stand taken by the Primitive Baptists:

> In the Primitive Baptist Church the literal teachings of the Bible were taken for daily living, and not only was a man responsible for himself, but was also his brother's keeper. All church members were expected to walk in the ways of God and to help their fellow men to do likewise. Should a brother or sister fall by the wayside, other church members came to the aid of the sinner and helped him or her repent; a man could be excommunicated for cheating or swindling his customers in business dealings, as well as for lying, swearing or getting drunk. He was expected to be ethical as well as moral in the strictest sense.[3]

This weapon of excommunication was utilized very effectively in Thomas County, as explained by William W. Rogers in *Antebellum Thomas County:* "In 1851 a white member was excommunicated for swearing and non-attendance at church. . . . Public humiliation by the church was enough to influence or at least moderate the behavior of the more exuberant citizens, and the church had public support when in 1860 it called upon one of its members to answer for indulging in the 'improper use of ardent spirits, and in the sin of gambling at the Billiard table in Thomasville.' "[4] One of the tales included in this section ("Turned Out of Church") satirizes not so much the strictness of excommunication as the inherent hypocrisy within it.

The minister or preacher, even though frequently uneducated

2. *Thomasville Times*, June 9, 1877, as quoted in William W. Rogers, *Thomas County, 1865–1900* (Tallahassee: Florida State University Press, 1973), p. 156.

3. Yvonne M. Brunton, *Grady County, Georgia: Some of its History, Folk Architecture, and Families* (Jackson, Mississippi: Quality Printers, 1979), p. 49.

4. William W. Rogers, *Antebellum Thomas County, 1825–1861* (Tallahassee: Florida State University Press, 1963), pp. 83–84.

(some merely heard "the call" and "went to preaching"), still held quite a revered position in the community. Rogers in *Thomas County, 1865–1900*, attested to the importance and influence of the minister: " 'There is no part of the world in which ministers of the Gospel are more respected,' a religious man believed, 'than in the Southern states.' "[5] The disparity between the ministry and the laity was substantial in the minds of the churchgoing populace. Although congregations would acknowledge that some ministers preached the gospel with more force and zeal than others, they were still slow to recognize and accept shortcomings in their man of God. But Grady Countians apparently relished humor that suggested foibles of the minister, for the tales collected here reflect such frailties as cursing, imbibing, vindictiveness, failure to pay debts on time, and cowardice.

Richard Dorson in his discussion of preachers in *American Negro Folktales* analyzed the basis for humor related to the church figure: "Through medieval and modern times, priest and parson have served as butts for innumerable lampoons, gibes and jests. Being learned and exalted figures, clothed in sanctity, yet dealing directly with the folk, clergymen formed natural targets for the satire of their less favored brethren. Their alleged pomposity, greed, unchastity, and hypocrisy made fine joke material for the humor of deflation and irreverence."[6]

28 · Dividing the Souls

Version A

Years ago before the forest was cut down and the trees cut out of the forest, a lot of hickory trees grew in this part of the country. And in the fall of the year, they had large hickory nuts

5. Kenneth K. Bailey, "Southern White Protestantism at the Turn of the Century," *American Historical Review* 68 (1963): 629, as quoted in Rogers, *Thomas County, 1865–1900*, p. 156.

6. Richard Dorson, *American Negro Folktales* (Greenwich, Conn.: Fawcett Publications, 1967), p. 363.

on them. So a lot of times the boys would go hickory nut hunting and pick up these hickory nuts. Of course, they were good to eat or bake cakes with—there were several things you could do with them.

Two little boys, they decided they wanted to go hickory nut hunting. So, they got them an old burlap bag apiece, and they went into the deep forest; under the hickory trees they found a lot of nuts, and they picked up. They weren't noticing the time; when they looked up, it was just about sundown, and they decided they better go home. So they started on home with their bag of hickory nuts, and they'd gone about a half a mile when they came to this old cemetery. Well, nobody hadn't been buried in there in a long time, and it was kind of thrown away, dilapidated. One little boy said to the other one, "Let's divide out our nuts here at this old cemetery."

The other little boy said, "Well, let's go inside the cemetery. There's a gate right here; we can go on the inside of the cemetery, and we'll sit down there on one of these graves. It will make a nice place to sit."

Now, the graves were just heaped-up clay—there wasn't much tombstone in the old cemetery. And as they went into the gate, the sack had a little hole in it, and two of the hickory nuts dropped out there at the gate. One of the little boys looked back and said, "Well, we dropped some here."

And the other one said, "Well, we'll get them as we come back out."

So, they went on in and picked them out a nice grave where the clay was heaped-up, and they sat down, just as it was about dusk dark. One little boy said, "You divide them out."

The other said, "Alright, I'm gonna do it like this: you take this'n, I'll take that'n; you take this'n, I'll take that'n; you take this'n, I'll take that'n; you take that'n, I'll take this'n."

They kept on dividing out the nuts, while in the meantime two Negro people came along the road. It was so dark, they couldn't see into the cemetery very well; but they heard the little boy in there saying, "You take this'n, I'll take that'n; you take this'n, I'll take that'n."

Well, one of them stopped and said, "What is that?"

104

The other one said, "I don't know, I don't know; but I don't like it."

And about that time the little boys finished counting out the hickory nuts; and one little boy said, "You remember, there's two at the gate now. You take one, and I'll take the other one."

Well, that was the last thing they wanted to hear, when the little boys said, "Two at the gate." Great goodness, they left that cemetery and run just as hard as they could and they were just scared to death. So they went on down the road, and they came to this house; and, well, it was getting dark, and the man who lived at the house saw them before they got there, just a-running. So he hollered and asked them, "What are y'all running for?"

They said, "Mister, the devil and God is down yonder in that cemetery, and they are sorting out the dead, we heard them. They were saying 'You take this'n, I'll take that'n.' We were standing there close to the gate, and after a while they said, 'You know, there's two at the gate. You take one, and I'll take the other one.' We left there; that was all we could stand. That's the reason we're running so."

Version B

I heard another one, one time, about two Irishmen coming along, and they come to a cemetery and stopped to rest. There was a grave just covered with pretty white shells. One said, "Well, that's one of the most prettiest things I've ever seen."

Another fellow come up; he said, "You know what these things is?"

One of the Irishmen said, "No, I've seen them before, but I don't know what they are."

So he told them, "Y'all just go ahead and look at them all you want to. I'm going to my neighbor's house up here; he's sick, and I'm going up there to see him."

He went on up there, and he told him about them Irishmen being down there resting. And he said, "I want you to go back down there with me."

The sick man said, "Man, you know I can't walk. I haven't taken a step in years. What you talking about me going?"

He said, "Well, I'll tote you."

He had something in his mind. They got back down to the gate of the cemetery; he got tired. He said, "I tell you, we'll sit down here and rest and then we'll go see where they're at."

The two Irishmen had decided that they'd get them shells, and one would take one, and one the other—they had a sack they were putting them in. When they got them all sacked up, one of them said to the other one, "This is all of them now, but them two at the gate. One of them's yours and one of them's mine."

That sick fellow that hadn't walked a step in years, he jumped up and beat the other fellow to the house.

29 · What Did Paul Say?

This happened years ago in the old horse-and-buggy days. This preacher was going to preach at his church, which wadn't far from where he lived. But before he left, he told his son, "Son, you go over to Mr. Paul Johnson's house and get us some sweet potatoes." Now, they'd been getting sweet potatoes from Mr. Johnson for some time. "After you get back home, you can get cleaned up and come on down to the church. I'm going on a little early."

So the little boy went over there after potatoes and came back without any, but, of course, his daddy didn't know that at the time. He got on his Sunday-go-to-meeting clothes and went on down to the church. His daddy was up in the pulpit preaching, and he was preaching about Paul. At a special point in the sermon he shouted, "An' what did Paul say?" He looked all around over the audience. Then he shouted again, "An' what did Paul say?" He happened to look right at his son, and the little boy thought he was talking to him.

He said, "Well, I tell you, Daddy, Paul said you couldn't get anymore sweet potatoes till you pay for those you already got."

30 · Preacher's Rabbit

The preacher was coming to eat dinner with this widow woman and her children, and they didn't have anything to eat; so the woman told the little boy, "Now the preacher is coming to our house for dinner. You go out and catch us a rabbit for dinner." The little boy, he went out, and he had a little dog with him. After a while, they jumped a rabbit; and the rabbit ran, and he ran into a hole in a hollow log right next to the road. The little boy, he ran his arm up in the hollow trying to get the rabbit, but he couldn't quite reach him. About that time a man came along in a buggy; of course, the little boy didn't know it, but it was the preacher that was supposed to eat dinner at his house that day. So the preacher stopped and said, "Howdy, son."

The boy said, "Good morning, sir."

"Son," the preacher said, "what you doing over there?"

"Well, my dog's got a rabbit treed in this hollow log."

"Well son, do you reckon you'll get him?"

"Yes sir," the boy answered, "I got to get him. Mama said that the preacher's gonna eat dinner at our house today, and we didn't have anything to eat; so, I've got to get this little rabbit."

The preacher said, "Get up! Get up! Get up!"

He went on down the road away from the widow woman's house and left the little boy down there after the rabbit.

31 · "Let Gabriel Blow His Horn"

Mama said that Preacher Blewett just told them that the black folks would just have such terrible preaching—just carry on so—that they wanted to see just what they would do if someone blowed the trumpet. So they climbed up in a tree near the church, and when the black preacher got in this big way of preaching—shouting something about the showposts of hell— he said something about blowing the trumpet for the gates of hell to be opened. Then the pranksters sat down on that horn and the people in the church went from there in a hurry. They said it was dinnertime the next day before they ever got the black folks back there to pick up their little children and their mules and wagons.

32 · Possum in the Church

Version A

I heard one about the black preacher that had church at night and said there was an old possum that got in his church. They didn't have no overhead ceiling—just a rafter—so this old possum was setting up there quiet. And the preacher said, "I want every head bowed while we have prayer." As he looked to the heavens to pray, he said, ▆▆▆▆▆▆▆▆, what a rat!"

Version B

This white man decided he'd play a joke on them black people, him and a couple more of the boys. So they caught a possum and put a little collar, or some kind of frilly something, around his neck, and put him up in the loft of the church. It didn't have no overhead ceiling, just some rafters; he could walk across them. The old preacher got to preaching, and that possum got to walking across there. The preacher looked up and saw him and hollered out, "Oh hell, what a dinky damn rat!"

33 · Mistletoe on the Preacher's Coattail

They told one about an old Negro preacher at this big Baptist church. He thought he had it made. But the deacons got together one night and called him in and said, "We want you to come prepared tonight to preach your farewell sermon." They said it made him so mad that he didn't know what to do. He walked in that church that night, got in the pulpit, and said, "Brothers and sisters, there ain't going to be no singing tonight." He said, "There ain't going to be no praying. In fact, there ain't going to be no preaching. There ain't going to be no nothing!" And he said, "I want all of you to take note of the mistletoe hanging to my coattail as I dart out this door for the last time."

34 · Jawbone of a Mule

You heard the one about the Negro preacher that couldn't think of nothing to say when he got in the pulpit, didn't you? He said that his friend was telling him, "Why don't you take a drink of liquor when you get up there? That will give you some conversation."

The preacher said, "Will that help?"

"Yeah."

He said, "I'm going to try it next Sunday."

Later, after he'd preached, he said, "How did I do?"

His friend said, "You preached a good sermon, but you sure fouled up that scripture."

"Why?" he asked.

His friend said, "That man didn't take the jawbone of a mule and beat the ass off of ten thousand people."

35 · The Nuns' Gasoline

They told about these four nuns who went out on their missions up in the mountains. The nuns was driving this old car that gave out of gas. So they went up to this farmhouse to see if they could get some gas. The old farmer said, "Well, I got gas, but I don't have nothing to put it in." They finally wound up with a bedpan and filled that full of gas. These four deacons drove up just as the nuns were pouring the gas in the car. The deacons said, "Sisters, could we help you?"

They said, "No, we have everything under control now."

One deacon said, "Well, I don't have but one thing to say: You got more faith than anybody I've ever seen."

36 · Turned Out of Church

Of course, I don't want to make fun of nobody's religion, but I heard one about the Primitive Baptists. Those Primitive Baptists had to have a vision before they'd let them become a member of that church. One lady had kept after her husband to have a vision. Well, he finally got up in the church, and his vision was that he dreamed that he was going across the heavens in a golden chariot with four white horses pulling it—that was his vision. So they took him in the church. When they was going back home—you know how women can be—the wife said, "John, did you really see a chariot with four white horses pulling it?"

He said, "Yeah."

Well, she kept on and after a while he said, "No, I didn't see no chariot. I just made it up to get in the church."

She said, "Well, we're going back next Sunday to retract that statement."

The next Sunday he got up and told the congregation that he'd just made it up to get in the church. So they voted right quick to turn him out. They asked him did he have anything to say. He said, "Yeah, I'd like to ask a question. Why do you take a man in the church for lying and then when he tells the truth, you turn him out?"

Tall Tales

Although the tall tale is usually considered the domain of Americans, such is not actually the case. Folklorists from Stith Thompson down to Richard Dorson have acknowledged a linkage to European tradition but have simultaneously questioned why so many of the interesting anecdotes failed to find a home in America. Jan Harold Brunvand in *The Study of American Folklore*, while recognizing European influence on some of the American tales, maintains that the number of tall tales from Europe is relatively few and cites some of the best-known "windies" found in the *Type-Index:* "Type 1889F, 'Frozen Words Thaw'; Type 1889L, 'The Split Dog'; Types 1890A through F, 'The Wonderful Hunt'; and Type 1920B, often called 'Too Busy to Tell a Lie'" (Brunvand, p. 115).

The tall tale, however, is extremely popular in the United States, with tales being found both in the oral tradition and in the jestbooks. Brunvand believes that the tales lose much in being relegated to the printed word, for the creativity of the yarn-spinner, when experienced firsthand, heightens the enjoyment of the tall tale.

37 · Corpse Sits Up in Coffin

They told about this fellow that was a little bit—well, they didn't think he had all that he was supposed to have, and they was going to scare him. They was going to have him set up with the dead—you know how they used to set up with the dead. They had this dead fellow that was deformed, and they had him tied in the casket. The pranksters kept turning these cats into the house. These cats would go walking through, but the fellow

113

setting up would just pat the cats as they'd go by; it didn't seem to bother him. One of the fellows eased under the casket and cut the rope tying the corpse down, and the dead man sat straight up in the casket. The fellow on watch said, "Lay back down, fellow. I'll keep the damn cats off of you." So they didn't scare him too much.

38 · The Giant Bedbug

An Englishman and a Southerner got to discussing what England had and what the United States had while this Englishman was staying over here. The man the Englishman was staying with never could get ahead of him. Whatever he might mention, they always had it in England, too. Now, the Southerner's kid had a pet terrapin, so before it was time to retire the man goes and puts it in the bed where the Englishman was going to sleep. After a while everybody got still, but the Englishman began to scream. The old man went tearing in there and said, "What in the world is the matter?"

"There's some kind of creature after me!"

The old man said, "That's only an American bedbug. Have you got anything like that in England?"

39 · Is the Corn Shucked?

This man lived in a small community. He wouldn't work; he wadn't no good at anything. So the people met to see what they could do. They decided to talk to him, but he just wouldn't work. One man said, "Let's bury him alive!" So they got him on the wagon to carry him to the place where he was to be buried. But one man felt sorry for him. "Let's don't do that," he said. "I'll give him a bushel of corn; he won't have to do anything."

The lazy man on the wagon turned around. "Is the corn shucked and shelled?"

"Well, no," the other man said.
"Well, drive on your wagon."

40 · Worms in the Mouth

This little black boy named Charlie, he was going fishing. So he dug him some worms, and he got his little cane pole and put over his shoulder, and he started down to the creek to go fishing. Before he got to the creek, he had to pass the neighbor's house, and his neighbor's name was Mr. Henry. Mr. Henry happened to be sitting on the porch. He said, "Charlie, where you going down the road?"

Charlie said, "I'm going down to the creek here. I'm going fishing."

He said, "Well, Charlie, what is that you got in your mouth?"

"It's worms," Charlies answered.

"Charlie," Mr. Henry said, "you got worms in your mouth! Why in the world don't you take them out and put them in your pocket?"

Charlie said, "Humph! You think I have them nasty things in there on my balca [tobacco]?"

41 · Ten Hens and a Rooster with One Shot

They said this fellow was kind of jumpy. He had a bunch of chickens that roosted in an old magnolia tree, out in front of the house. Well, something got after them one cold night, and his wife tried to get him to get up and see about his chickens— he's one that wore them old long johns. He got out his shotgun, and he eased along back there. Then his old bird dog slipped up behind him and touched him on the fanny. They say he shot up in the tree and killed ten hens and a rooster.

42 · The Coon-Monkey

This fellow had a coon-monkey. What he done, he was down here in Florida and he'd trained monkeys to work with the coonhounds. He was up here in north Georgia delivering, and he had the coon-monkey in the cab of the truck with him. He stopped to get gas at this station, and the owner said, "Hey, what you got there?"

Said, "That's a coon-monkey."

"Coon-monkey!?"

"Yeah, he works with the coonhounds and they are good. I mean all coon hunters should have one."

The owner said, "Hey fellow, what does the monkey do?"

"Well, he helps the dog get the coon out of the tree. Where you got a lot of Spanish moss, oh, you just don't beat them now. They're it. You couldn't hardly do without them."

"Well, look, I got a couple of dogs, and I'm interested."

He said, "Are you?"

"Yeah, I'll train them and sell them. Look, if you ain't in no big hurry, I'd love for you to stay over for a couple hours. We got plenty of coons, and we have trouble about getting them out of the tree. I'd like to see them work."

The coon-monkey's owner said, "Well, okay, I could put on a demonstration."

He said, "Well, come on, let's go to the house and eat supper, and we'll go down to the river there and see them work."

So they went and had supper and took off to the river; sure 'nuff, they turned the dogs loose and in a few minutes they'd treed a coon. This fellow unleashed his monkey, reached in his pocket, and give him a .38; he said, "Go git him." Right up that tree the coon-monkey went and—"pow!"—the coon hit the ground. The monkey come down. The man said, "That's his job."

Fellow said, "Good! Now, doggone, this is something. I'm telling you this is something. But I got a neighbor that's got some dogs." And he said, "You got the monkey sold?"

He said, "Yeah."

"Well, look, did you tell him when you was gonna bring the monkey?"

He said, "No."

"Well, let me have this one. I really want him. Sell this one to me and bring him another one. I got a neighbor over there that's got some dogs, and I want him to see this monkey work."

"All right. I hate to do the man that-a-way, though. I get $100 for the monkey."

The other man said, "I'll give you $150 and you just leave him with me and go and bring him another one."

"Well, in that case I might just do that." So he did. He said, "Now one thing. I was about to forget that. I'm selling them so fast and training them so fast, but there's nothing perfect; if anything, anything at all goes wrong, here's my phone number—you call me. I'll correct it."

"Okay, that's good enough, good enough."

So he left the monkey and went on back to Florida. Training more monkeys, you know.

The other man's neighbor come down the next day, and the man said, "Hey, I got a coon-monkey, boy. Now this here is out of this world."

"Now what's he do?" the neighbor asked.

"He climbs the tree and gets us the coon. Just like that. Now if you want to, we'll get your dogs and go try them out tonight."

The neighbor said, "Good, I want to see that."

So he said, "Now my boy is going to be using my dogs. We'll take your dogs, and I'll carry the monkey. We'll go over there where the Spanish moss is. I really want you to see how this baby here works."

That night, they went a way up the river where the Spanish moss was; they turned the dogs out, and they run, barking and a-running, barking and a-running, and barking and a-running for about thirty or forty minutes, until they'd settled on one tree. The man took the leash off the monkey, reached in his back pocket, and handed him the .38. Up the tree he went. He stayed up in the tree about five minutes. They shined the light up there a little bit, and they seen the monkey pass out of that tree into another one. The man said, "Well, that's unusual." Stayed up there about three or four minutes, and he'd pass out of that tree into another one. He went into three or four or five trees around there and come back down. Walked up to the neighbor's best

117

coon dog and—"pow!"—shot him and killed him! He said, "Oh, my God! What has gone wrong with that fool monkey! My goodness, nothing like this, nothing like this. But he give me the phone number to call him. Let's run back to the station; I'll call him now. Man, he's done killed your best dog."

He got on long distance, and he called the man that was training the monkey. He said, "Hey, something done gone wrong up here."

"What's that?"

"I'm the guy that you sold the monkey to."

He said, "Yeah?"

"We took him out tonight, and he went up a tree and stayed fifteen or twenty minutes, passing around from one tree to another one up there, and come down and shot my neighbor's best dog."

"Oh, by heck," he said, "I forgot to tell you that. Now if there's anything that that monkey hates worse that a coon, it's a lying dog! There wasn't no coon up there."

43 · Underground Woodpecker

O ne day I was digging this well for some neighbors of mine. Well, we got down to about forty feet and struck sumpin' hard. I hollered up to the fellow who was drawing dirt out of the hole to send me down the axe. By that time I had scratched away the dirt and discovered that it was an old hollow log. I hit a few licks with my axe, and out came the biggest, orneriest woodpecker you ever did see!

44 · The Hard Rain

T he children had been playing with this barrel which was out in the yard with the bunghole up; both ends of the barrel were gone. Well, when I went out on the porch to look, it was raining so hard in the bunghole that the water could not get out both ends and was just spewing up from the bunghole. After the rain stopped, I went out in the yard and picked up a mess of fish from around the barrel.

45 · Mule Almost Drowns in Mud-hole

Not far from where we lived we came to where the road bent sharp around this fence corner. This man had just fenced in his field. And when a man fenced in his field, he tried to take in every corner that was his. Consequently, the wagons and buggies had to turn real short to pass one at a time. The wheels had dug out a hole, and, as it held water, hogs had wallowed in it so much that it became boggy. The law of Georgia at that time said each man had to give back six feet from the land line.

Well, Sol Whitfield had loaded his wagon to go to the coast for a load of salt fish. He was driving two small mules. The hole was wallowed out so big that his wagon tongues stuck in the bank of the hole and broke. And one mule bogged down and almost drowned.

46 · Suicide Attempt with Carbolic Acid

I'd be like the fellow that went to the hardware store and bought a rope to cross the river, a .38 and a bottle of carbolic acid. He went out and stretched his rope across the river and walked out there on his hands. When he got out there, he drank his carbolic acid, got out his revolver with the other hand, and shot the rope in two. He fell in the river and drank muddy water. It made him sick and he lost his carbolic acid. They said that if he hadn't been a good swimmer, he'd 've drowned.

Other Tales and a Novella

47 · Nothing Except the Fence

This happened years ago. Back then, a lot of people in the community, especially farmers, were poor, and they were working a crop on shares—well, we called it on halves—for the landowner. One little boy, he was out plowing corn aside of the fence, and the corn did look mighty bad; they didn't use much fertilizer. This traveling salesman came by in a horse-drawn buggy, and since he wadn't in a hurry, he just decided he'd stop and talk to this boy a little bit. He said, "Whoa, Maude!" and the horse stopped. The little boy was plowing the end of the row, and the salesman said, "Well, howdy, son."

The boy said, "Howdy do, sir?"

So the salesman said, "Well, I was just passing by and decided I'd stop and talk with you a little bit."

The little boy said, "Well, I'm glad you did. I'm a little tired myself, and I need a rest here."

"Son, just looking at your corn, it looks mighty yellow."

"Yes sir, we planted the yellow kind."

"Well, son, I don't believe you gonna make no more than a half crop of corn, no way."

The little boy said, "No sir, that's all we working for—just a half crop."

"Son," the salesman said, "you know something? There's not much difference between you and a fool, are there?"

"No sir, nothing except a fence."

So that traveling salesman, he said, "Get up there, Maude!" And he hit the old horse with his switch and down the road they went.

48 · Sheephead and Dumplings

This happened years ago in the old horse-and-buggy days. There was a widow woman and she lived not far from the church, not more than about half a mile. They had preaching only on Saturday, so she told her little boy, "You stay here and watch what I'm going to put on for dinner. I'm going to put on this pot here, and it has a sheephead in it." You know, back then they ate the sheep's head too. So she put the sheephead in a big pot and told the little boy, "Now you keep a fire under here and keep it going. I'm going to the church, and by the time preaching's over, why, it'll be cooked. I'll be back soon, and we'll have dinner." So the little boy told her he would.

Well, the little boy got along fine, but after a while, though—now this was an old wooden stove they were cooking on—he wadn't noticing what kind of wood he was putting in, and he got ahold of some fatwood. Now, fatwood makes a big fire, a lot more than usual. So he put the fatwood in the stove, and the pot commenced to boiling all over the stove. He didn't know what to do, so the first thing he thought to do was to run to the church and tell his mama.

He ran as hard as he could to the church, but he wouldn't go in 'cause he wadn't cleaned up; he had on his dirty clothes. But he went to the door of the church where he thought he could see his mama. And he did. She was sitting up in the old women's pew, and the preacher, he was a-preaching as hard as he could. And he was one of these long-winded, pot-liquor preachers. So the little boy, he winked at his mama. She shook her head and winked wildly back at him so he would go away. He winked again and so did she. But she wouldn't come. He didn't know what else to do. All of a sudden he just blurted out, "Mama, you can sit over there and wink and blink if you want to, but that sheephead is butting all them dumplings out of the pot."

49 · The Obstinate Wife

This farmer and his wife lived out a piece from town in the country. And, of course, back then the husband generally went to town once a week on Saturday evening. And she would send for what groceries and other things they needed.

So, she wanted a pair of scissors, and she would put them on the list. Well, he would leave off the scissors every week. She would put them on there again, and he would leave off the scissors. Then she got to telling him, when he started to town, "Be sure and get my scissors now: I need them." And he would go to town and would forget them again. So she kept on after him, and he got to where it would just make him mad every time she would mention scissors.

So finally, one day, he told his wife, "I've heard scissors and scissors and scissors every time I started to town for so long; if you say "scissors" to me once more, I'm gonna drown you!"

Well, it made her mad, and she said, "Scissors."

He said, "Well, I just as well to go ahead and drown you." He held her down so long she couldn't quite get her head up above the water, so she stuck these two fingers up like two scissor blades and did like this when she was going down the last time. She got in the last word.

50 · Bundle of Twigs

Version A

There was a man who had seven sons. He'd sit down every night after supper on the porch. He'd tell them that as long as they stayed together, there was nobody that could break them. One day he proved it to them. He got him seven sticks and bundled them all up together. He handed the bundle to every one of them and told each one to break the bundle. They couldn't do it. Then he separated the bundle and handed each son a separate stick. Each one broke his stick. "Now if you stay together, nobody can break you, but if you fall apart, you can be broken like the stick."

Version B
(printed in the *Cairo Messenger*, August 14, 1908)

The old man called his son to him to explain the mysteries of business. "My son," said he, "you have finished college and you must now make a show at least of getting busy. Let me explain to you a few fundamentals. Here I have a bundle of sticks. See if you can break them." The young man had been absent from school with appendicitis at the time his class read the old story of the bundle of sticks. He tried and tried to break the sticks, but could not. "See how easy it is," said the old man, taking the sticks, cutting the cord and breaking them one by one.

"Gee, that's a bum joke," said the young man, as he puffed his cigarette and tried to look interested.

"It's no joke," said the old man. "It is a parable. The bundle of sticks taken together represent organization, which is very desirable in the use of capital. If, however, we look upon the sticks as representing labor, it is criminal and immoral for them to be tied together. Always keep your capital sticks tied together and your labor sticks separate."

"I should think what's sauce for the goose is sauce for the gander," said the son, whose point of view was still blunt.

"It depends on how big a goose you are," replied the old man.

Notes to the Tales

1 · Racing a Ghost

Motif J1495.1: "*Man runs from actual or supposed ghost. The ghost runs beside him. The man stops to rest; the ghost stops, says, 'That was a good run we had!' The man says, 'Yes, and as soon as I get my breath, I'm going to run some more.'*"

Motif J1495.3: "*Man attempts to stay in haunted house all night. Ghost tells him, 'There ain't nobody here but you and me.' Man says, 'And I ain't going to be here long.'*"

Informant: William Robert Glenn, May 6, 1972

This tale with its wide distribution in the United States embraces several motifs in its numerous variants: J1495.1, J1495.3 (given above), J1495.2 "When Caleb comes," and J1495.4 "Man racing with ghost outruns rabbit." Combinations or hybrids of all kinds exist in the reporting of this tale. Richard Dorson in his headnote "Waiting for Rufus" concludes that "variations on a comic tale of frights that scare a man from a haunted house circulate widely in American white and Negro traditions." Furthermore, he states that "believed tales of haunted houses have generated this very popular folktale, an American oikotype of Type 326, 'The Youth Who Wanted to Learn What Fear Is'" (*American Negro Folktales* [New York: Fawcett World Library, 1968], pp. 320–21).

The Grady County tale incorporates motifs J1495.1 and J1495.3, omitting motifs pertaining to waiting for Caleb (or Rufus) or to outrunning a rabbit. Some of the variants which, likewise, utilize these same two motifs and which are more closely aligned in descriptive details with the Grady County tale are those from West Virginia (Cox), North Carolina (Boggs), South Carolina (Fuller), Alabama (informants from

Virginia and North Carolina), Philadelphia (informants from Virginia and North Carolina), and Indiana (Meese, informant from Kentucky).[1]

Whereas in many of the variants there is an enticement or a reward (meat, gold, watermelons, money) for staying in the haunted house, in the Grady County version there is only a traveling salesman looking for a place to stay the night. Frequently, the visitor is named (Uncle Mose, John, Uncle Tom, Rastus, Mr. Joe, Mr. Peters, Edgar Miner, Charlie Buckalew); other times he is simply the preacher, the man, the colored boy, the brother-in-law, or the salesman. In some of the Southern variants, a cat is the means of inducing fear by stating, "Dey ain't nobody heah but me an' you." In the variant from Grady County the black cat serves merely as a presage for the real terrors: ice-cold hands on the neck and a deep, ghostly voice delivering in a slow cadence the refrain "There ain't nobody here but me and you." The shift then to the rapidly stated reply of the frightened man serves to heighten the humor and relieve the tension: "No, and if you wait till I get on my pants, there won't be nobody here but you!" (For a study of the suprasegmental phonemes in an Indiana variant, see Meese, "The Art of the Tale Teller," pp. 25–37.) In a variant from the Sea islands, South Carolina, it is the talking mule, Jack, which scares the man and causes him to run (see also Zora Hurston, *Mules and Men* [Philadelphia: 1935], pp. 131–32, for a similar version). And in John H. Johnson's "Folk-Lore from Antigua, British West Indies" (*JAF* 34 [1921]: 70), the man comes home after seven years to be frightened by talking peas, okra, dogs, and wood.

The Grady County tale is laced with details which definitely place it in the past—"old horse-and-buggy days," "kerosene lamps," "horse in the lot," the absence of "hotels and motels as they have now." Few of the tales are embellished with as much description as Mr. Glenn gives in his variant.

Several notes are of special interest. Herbert Halpert ("Folktales and Legends from the New Jersey Pines: A Collection and a Study," Ph.D. diss. [Indiana University, 1947], p. 686) states that the form of this story which incorporates "Wait till Caleb comes" has been used by stage comedians and newspaper cartoonists. Halpert, in his following note on "Outracing the Rabbit" (p. 687), gives a variant by Lincoln in

1. John H. Cox, "Negro Tales from West Virginia," *JAF* 47 (1934): 355–56; Ralph S. Boggs, "North Carolina White Folktales and Riddles," *JAF* 47 (1934): 318; Elizabeth A. Meese, "The Art of the Tale Teller: A Study of the Suprasegmental Phonemes in a Folktale," *Kentucky Folklore Record* 14 (1968): 31–37.

Sandburg's biography, 2:296. John H. Cox suggests that the story has a minstrel heritage: "One of the commonest types of vaudeville jokes about the Negro, probably of white origin, is the joke in which the frightened Negro outruns various fleet animals and comments on or to them as he passes" (p. 355). Cox refers to a similar story in verse from Alabama given in Newman I. White's *American Negro Folk Songs* (Cambridge: Harvard University Press, 1928), p. 205. The middle portion of the tale is strongly reminiscent of the Grady County tale:

> When midnight a spooky said,
> "Now Sam, we're all alone."
> "Don't make dat WE so strong," says Sam
> While reaching for the shelf;
> "Jus' let me get my clothes on, dear
> An' you'll be by yo'se'f,
> Cause it ain' no disgrace to run
> When you git skeered."

This tale is also part of the Anansi tradition, the spider trickster of a large body of West African folktales (Leach, *Standard Dictionary of Folklore, Mythology, and Legend,* p. 52). It emerges as a Duppy story in Martha W. Beckwith's "Jamaica Anansi Stories" and as a Mis' Nancy in a variant from the Sea islands, South Carolina (*Memoirs of the American Folklore Society* 17 [1924]: 180; 16 [1923]: 71–73).

There are interesting endings on both the Grady County tale and the fourth variant from the Sea islands, South Carolina (p. 73). Arthur Huff Fauset in his article "Negro Folk Tales from the South" (*JAF* 40 [1927]: 214), discusses briefly the formal beginnings and endings to black stories. He suggests an ending used quite frequently:

> I stepped on a piece of tin
> The tin bended
> My story ended.

The Sea island variant is quite similar: "He step on a pin, and the pin ben'/ And now my story is end." In the Grady County tale, Mr. Glenn ends his story as he does frequently, with this explanation: "I couldn't hang around because I had on paper clothes, and I was afraid the wind might blow or it might rain."

This tale certainly bears out Elsie Clews Parsons's assessment as given in her "Tales From Guilford County, North Carolina" (*JAF* 30 [1917]: 168). Earlier in her commentary she was lamenting that the art of the folktale was in its last stage of disintegration. But she alluded to this tale, which she called "The Black Cat," when she said that "some of the tales appear to be holding their own more than others."

2 · Ghost of a Baby

Informant: Allen Womble, August 17, 1972

No exact parallel to this tale could be found in Baughman. Several motifs, however, are evident: E422.1.11.4 "Revenant as skeleton," E425.3 "Revenant as child," and E402.1.1.3 "Ghost cries and screams." The setting of the tale makes use of local history in describing the preparation needed for a three-day trip to the coast in a covered wagon (see Introduction for detailed information on this custom). The beginning is reminiscent of Mr. Glenn's tale "Racing a Ghost," where the man searches for a place to stay and is warned of the haunted house; he ultimately sees a black cat which presages the ghost that is to come.

3 · Ghost Gives Pot of Gold

Motif E371.4: "Ghost of man returns to point out buried treasure."

Informant: Athelone Barrett, March 21, 1976

In addition to motif E371.4, which parallels the Grady County variant, Baughman lists motif E371.5 where the benevolent ghost is a woman. Several motifs, however, are contained in this one tale: H1411 "Fear test: staying in haunted house"; E545.19.2 "Proper means of addressing ghosts"; and E545.12 "Ghost directs man to hidden treasure."

Richard Dorson in his headnote to tale 114 in *American Negro Folktales* links this tale to black lore: "Buried treasure revealed by spirits in dreams or visions constitutes a large section of Negro belief tales, although Baughman gives only two Negro references" (p. 228).

This tale certainly seems to have a strong European tradition with eight of the variants coming from Ireland, Wales, Scotland, and various places in England. Very few commonalties, however, exist among the variants aside from the previously cited motifs. Perhaps one reason for such variance is that many of the tales are told as local legends, such as the Money Cave legend from Canada.

Some similarities are fairly strong, however. In most of the United States variants there is a "fear test" where the person who shows courage (by staying in a haunted house and following the spirit) reaps the reward of buried treasure. In the same headnote to tale 114, Dorson cites a section from the *Southern Workman* clarifying a point on black ghost lore: "The ghost in Negro folklore is a being that is often misunderstood. If he is met with courage he regards those who speak to him, as he is in many cases, the guardian of concealed treasure" (vol. 27, no. 3 [March 1898]: 57).

Many of the variants allude to the proper way of addressing or confronting a ghost: reading a passage from the Bible backward in front of a mirror, making the sign of the cross, using the name of God or the Holy Spirit, or simply addressing the ghost first to prove lack of fear. While many of the variants do incorporate the person's speaking first to the ghost, the Spanish tale from Texas explains the folk belief inherent in this practice: "As all Christian people know, a ghost cannot speak to a living person unless the person speaks first" (Charles L. Sonnichsen, "Mexican Spooks from El Paso," *Publications of Texas Folklore Society* 13 [1937]: 122).

Some details in the tales suggest possible dates that the "buried treasure" motif was in existence, such as in the Skinner variants from New York and Ohio (Charles M. Skinner, *Myths and Legends of our Own Land* [Philadelphia: 1896], 1:104–6 and 109–12; 2:110–12). In one of his tales it is "Gouveneur Morris, American minister to the court of Louis XVI," who returns as a ghost in 1817 to his widow. In his other variant New Amsterdam, rather than New York, is the name of the city.

4 · The Ghost of Rit Hayes's Wife

Informant: William Robert Glenn, May 6, 1972

"Rit Hayes's Ghost," although told purely as a factual incident, incorporates two motifs: E332.3.1 "Ghost rides on horseback with rider" and E581.2 "Dead person rides horse." William Montell gives five variants of this tale, one of which (variant C) parallels the Grady County variant somewhat. Here the dead wife returns to ride on the mule behind her husband who had mistreated her in life (*Ghosts along the Cumberland* [Knoxville: University of Tennessee Press, 1975], pp. 119–120).

5 · How to Become a Witch

Motif G224.13.2: "Initiation: person kneels, puts one hand under feet, other on head, says: 'All that's between my hands belongs to Satan.'"

Informant: Allen Womble, August 17, 1972

Vance Randolph gives a variant of this tale which dates back at least to 1889 and which many people regard as a true story (*Who Blowed Up the Church House and Other Ozark Folk Tales* [New York: Columbia University Press, 1952], pp. 119–21, 213). Randolph also gives a variant out of Missouri, citing the article "Burning Witches in Missouri," *Kansas City Post*, January 16, 1916. Other variants have been collected, however, in both Kentucky and North Carolina. In most of the tales the instructions to the new recruit include placing one hand under the feet and the other on top of the head and repeating the refrain "All that's between my hands belongs to Satan." In the variants from Arkansas, Kentucky, and Georgia, the initiate repeats the first phrase but substitutes the Lord's name for that of the devil. With the utterance of the word *Lord*, all of the witches disappear, and the initiate finds herself (or himself) back in some normal environment—an empty house (Arkansas), a "bunch of thorn trees" (Kentucky), or an old cotton house (Georgia).[2] In the Kentucky and Arkansas variants the new recruit makes contact with a supposed witch at a quilting bee and proceeds to be initiated by a female witch. In the tale from North Carolina it is a man (Ferro) who bewitches people and tries to initiate Eph' Tucker into the cult (*The Frank C. Brown Collection of North Carolina Folklore* [Durham: Duke University Press, 1952], 1:648–49). Here Eph' must step into a ring drawn in the dirt and repeat the magic phrase. The Georgia narrator, likewise, ascribes the name of Ila Gilly to his witch and places the setting of her tales in Bancroft, Georgia. The Georgia variant includes many more details in the prelude to the initiation than do the other tales: an account of magical abilities of witches, a description of the palatial fairy-tale tower where the ceremony is held, elaborate details of the old witch with her diamond-studded wand, and even some dialogue from the assemblage of witches in urging on the initiate. In each of the variants, however, the chant required for witchhood is

2. Randolph, *Who Blowed Up the Church House*, pp. 119–21, 213; Elizabeth B. Cornett, "Down Our Way: Belief Tales of Knott and Perry Counties," *Kentucky Folklore Record* 2 (1956): 71.

never repeated, and the recruit is cured of her or his desire to become a witch.

6 · Witch Rider

Motif G211.1.1.2: "Witch as horse shod with horseshoes"

Motif G241.2.1: "Witch transforms man to horse and rides him"

Informant: Allen Womble, August 17, 1972

Motifs G211.1.1.2 and G241.2.1 are the most significant elements in the Grady County tale. The bridle, although the primary means of transformation in many of the variants, is only implied in the Georgia tale. Here it is a magic chant that the witch uses to transform the boy; in turn, the same chant is used upon her: "Lickty-skip and here we go."

The blacksmith, however, is paramount in most of the variants. Emelyn E. Gardner suggests reasons for the importance of the smith and his iron works: "But in the mythologies of many peoples the idea is widespread that the art of the smith was first discovered and practiced by supernatural personages, who through their art had great power over the forces of evil. Such were Culann, the mystic smith of Celtic folklore, Hephaestus of Greek mythology, Thor of Teutonic mythology, and Wayland Smith of Scottish tradition. . . . The belief in the power of iron against evil spirits may go back to a period in human culture, perhaps the stone age, when iron was still a novelty, and smiths were looked upon as magicians. . . . It has been suggested that the horseshoe may have gained sanctity from the presence of the horse and the ass in the stall where Christ was born" (*Folklore from the Schoharie Hills, New York* [Ann Arbor: University of Michigan Press, 1937], p. 65). Richard Dorson, in his headnote to tale 120, "Witching-Riding," alludes to the use of the horseshoe as a means of warding off witches: "A horseshoe over the door makes a witch traverse the road covered by the horse" (*American Negro Folktales*, quoted in Mary W. Minor, "How to Keep Off Witches [as related by a Negro]," *JAF* 2 [1895]: 76).

George L. Kittredge refers to the practice of witch riding numerous times in *Witchcraft in Old and New England* (Cambridge: Harvard University Press, 1929), citing some cases where it occurred: "The Norse hero Vanlandi was ridden to death by 'the mare' while his men stood by and could see nothing, although they did their best to help him" (p. 219). Another example that Kittredge uses is the actual case of Edmund

Robinson, a small boy of ten or eleven who lived near the area of the Lancashire witches of 1612: "Goody Dickinson, he testified, had carried him off on a white horse (which was a boy transformed by a magic bridle) to a house in the neighborhood. There he saw divers persons about the door, and others came riding up 'on Horses of several colours'" (p. 270).

Kittredge later alludes to Robinson's stories as lies but points out that they serve as excellent evidence of the folk beliefs of the times (p. 271).

7 · Witch as a Hog

Motif G211.1.6: "Witch as hog"

Informant: Allen Womble, August 17, 1972

The distribution of this tale seems to suggest strongly a British as well as a New England heritage. George L. Kittredge attests to the popularity of the metamorphosis belief: "From Elizabeth's accession to the present moment the witch-creed has cherished the notion that demons may have the form of animals, and that in this guise they may serve the witch as familiar spirits to carry out her wicked designs. Or the witch may transform herself into beast-shape; then if the animal is wounded, she suffers in like manner" (p. 174).

8 · The Ass's Egg

Type 1319: "Pumpkin Sold as Ass's Egg"

Motif J1772.1: "Pumpkin thought to be ass's egg"

Informant: M. P. Maxwell, August 13, 1972

In 1946 Stith Thompson listed this anecdote as having considerable popularity in various folk traditions. "This anecdote not only appears in Turkish jestbooks, but is told all over Europe, in much of Asia, and among mountain whites in Virginia" (*The Folktale*, p. 190). The tale has now been reported in Canada and many sections of the United States: New Jersey, Virginia, North Carolina, Mississippi, Texas, Arkansas, Kentucky, Ohio, Indiana, Idaho, and even as far west as California.

Having a literary heritage as well as an oral one, this tale can be traced back to at least the early eighteenth century. William Clouston in *The Book of Noodles* gives two variants from literary sources: Riviere's French collection of tales of the Kabail, Algeria, and the *Gooroo Paramartan*, an amusing work in the Tamil language by Beschi, a missionary in India from 1700 until 1742 (pp. 29, 37–38). The Indian version is quite similar to most of the variants reported in the United States with the substitution of the "Gooroo" for the Irishman; the Algerian version, however, uses a watermelon rather than a pumpkin and makes no mention of a rabbit.

Most of the variants reported in the United States and Canada do incorporate the Irishman as the numskull. Occasionally, there are variations, such as a green city-boy or a country man pulling fodder. The appearance of the rabbit or hare when the pumpkin bursts occurs in most variants. And even in the Irishman's call to his supposed newly hatched colt in the several variants, there is some similarity: "Koop, coltie, here's your mammy"; "Cope, cope, cope! Go on you little devil"; "Cope, cope, cope, here's yore mammy"; Coltie, coltie, nice coltie." Whatever the call, the numskull in his absurd misunderstanding of the situation usually labels himself the "mammy" of the rabbit-colt. The Grady County variant differs in its ending: the Irishman thinks, when he sees the rabbit's ears, that he has gotten an ass instead of a horse.

9 · Hanging for Water

Type 1250: "Bringing Water from the Well." See also type 1336 "Diving for Cheese" and type 34 "The Wolf Dives into the Water for Reflected Cheese."

Motif J2133.5: "Men hang down in a chain until top man spits on his hands. A log is laid across the top of the well. One man holds to the log with his hands, the next climbs down and holds to his feet, and so on; the uppermost man becomes tired and lets go to spit on his hands." Baughman (1966) notes that "all the Canadian and United States variants . . . except the one from Florida, include the motif of recovering the moon from the well." See also J1791.3 "Diving for cheese."

Informant: William Robert Glenn, May 6, 1972

This type of numskull story, where the fool needlessly risks his life, is not very common in oral tradition, according to Thompson in *The*

Folktale. He suggests that only two tales of this type are widely told: one involving men "who hang down in a chain until the top man spits on his hands and they all fall"; the other featuring the fool who saws off the branch upon which he is sitting (p. 193). The heritage of both types goes back as far as oriental history sources. William Clouston in *The Book of Noodles* (1888) gives several variants of "Bringing Water from the Well," concluding that the "germ of all stories of this class is perhaps found in the *Jatakas,* or Buddist Birth Stories: a pair of geese resolve to migrate to another country and agree to carry with them a tortoise, their intimate friend, taking the ends of a stick between the bills, and the tortoise grasping it by the middle with his mouth. As they are flying over Benares, the people exclaim in wonder to one another at such a strange sight, and the tortoise, unable to maintain silence, opens his mouth to rebuke them, and by so doing falls to the ground and is dashed to pieces" (pp. 52–53). Kurt Ranke, editor of *Folktales of Germany* (Folktales of the World Series [University of Chicago Press, 1966]) noted that this anecdote was found in the German *Lalebuch* toward the end of the sixteenth century and that the motif of the human (or animal) chain is given in early combinations, "as in the Chinese *Tripitaka,* where the chain of monkeys hanging on a branch try to get the moon out of the well, or in the Indian *Kathasaritsagara*" (p. 229). Ranke acknowledges the popularity of this tale in Asia, Europe, and both Americas; thirty versions from Germany are reported.

With very few exceptions most of the variants combine type 1250 "Bringing Water from the Well" with type 1336 "Diving for Cheese" (see also type 34), and motif J2133.5, "Men hang down in a chain" with J1791.3 "Diving for cheese." The exceptions include variants from Germany, Zuni and Creek Indians, Miami, and now Georgia. A few of the variants use combinations of type 1287 where the numskulls (after they fall into the water) are unable to count their own number, place noses in mud, and count the imprints. The tale from Miami (Elsie Clews Parsons, "Folk-Tales Collected at Miami, Florida," JAF 30 [1917]: 222–23) is more closely related to the Grady County variant.

10 · Mistaken Identity

Informant: William Robert Glenn, May 6, 1972

This short anecdote is closely akin to motif J1485 "Mistaken identity" although it does not parallel Baughman's example. Melville Landon's version in *Wit and Humor of the Age* (Chicago: Star Publishing Co., 1894), pp. 278–79, however, is almost identical to the Grady County variant.

11 · Carrying Part of the Load

Type 1242A: "Carrying Part of the Load. A rider takes the meal-sack on his shoulder to relieve the ass of his burden."

Motif J1874.1: "Rider takes the meal-sack on his shoulders to relieve the ass of his burden."

Informant: William Robert Glenn, May 6, 1972.

Like several stories in the Grady County collection, this tale shares both an oral and a literary heritage, having appeared in nineteenth-century jestbooks such as Clouston's *The Book of Noodles* (1898) and *Shakespeare's Jest-Books*, ed. William C. Hazlitt (London: 1864). Melville Landon in *Wit and Humor of the Age* assigns this repartee to the class of thoughtless blunder or a bull where the abuse falls upon the speaker himself (p. 268).

Clouston, in his discussion of the history of this tale, indicated that the tale had a much earlier oral and literary circulation than the nineteenth century, however. One early tradition in which it was found was the Gothamite stories, passed down from the people in "a village in Nottinghamshire—who are credited with most of the noodle stories which have been current among the people for centuries past, though other places share to some extent in their not very enviable reputation" (p. 16). But even before the men of Gotham were held up as fools, Clouston maintained that similar stories had been told of men of Norfolk dating back to the twelfth century. As to this particular tale Clouston made the statement "The well-known Gothamite jest of the man who put a sack of meal on his own shoulders to save his horse, and then got on the animal's back and rode home, had been previously told of a man of Norfolk" (p. 19).

The tale then appeared in *Bigarrures; or, the Pleasant and Witless and Simple Speeches of the Lord Gaulard of Burgundy*, a translation of Etienne Tabourot's *Les Contes facetieux de Sieur Gaulard*, written in the sixteenth century. Tabourot, according to Clouston, "is said to have written the tales in ridicule of the inhabitants of Franche Comte, who were then subjects of Spain and reputed to be stupid and illiterate" (p. 8).

In another example of the tale from Clouston, a Singhalese variant from Ceylon has been reduced to a proverb (pp. 67–68). C. J. R. le Mesurier, a learned writer on proverbial lore of the Singhalese, wrote in *The Orientalist* (Kandy, Ceylon: 1884): "The story is of the double-fool—i.e., of the man who tried to lighten the boat by carrying his pingo over his shoulders" (quoted in Clouston, pp. 67–68).

12 · Mule Wants to Ride

Type 1329: "Mounted Numskull Thinks Mule Wants to Ride"

Motif J1818.2: "Ass kicks at flies, gets foot caught in the stirrup. The rider says, 'Faith, if you're going to get up, it's time I was getting down.'" See also J2259(b) "Rider is hit in the back with a rock as he rides on mule. He curses mule for kicking him."

Informant: William Robert Glenn, October 1974

This noodle tale has parallels in Clouston's *Book of Noodles*, and in Leonard Roberts's *South from Hell-fer-Sartin: Kentucky Mountain Tales* (Berea, Kentucky: The Council of Southern Mountains, 1964), pp. 126–27, 253. Both variants are almost identical to the Grady County tale. James Whitmore in his monologue on Truman, *Give 'Em Hell, Harry* (filmed performance shown in Tallahassee during September 1974), incorporated the Truman quip on Lincoln's admonition to General George B. McClellan: "If you want up, I'll get down."

Clouston cites an analogous jest to this tale from Henry Stephens's introduction to his *Apology for Herodotus*, published in London in 1607 (a separate work from the *Apologie pour Herodote*): "He [Stephens] tells of a fellow who was hit on the back with a stone as he rode upon his mule, and curses the animal for kicking him" (p. 119).

13 · Outrunning the Train

Informant: Elmer Wilcox, August 3, 1976

This tale incorporates motif J2259 "Absurd lack of logic: miscellaneous." No exact parallel exists in Baughman.

14 · Green Persimmons

Informant: William Robert Glenn, May 6, 1972

The tale, though having no exact parallel in Baughman, shares some kinship with motif K1043 where "the dupe is induced to eat sharp (stinging, bitter) fruit." Perhaps a new subdivision could be added to type 1339 "Strange Foods": type GA 1339F "Fool is Unacquainted with Persimmons."

15 · Crossing the Stream

Informant: William Robert Glenn, May 6, 1972

"Crossing the Stream" utilizes motif J2259 "Absurd lack of logic: miscellaneous." No exact parallel exists in Baughman.

16 · The Blind Fiancée

Type 1456: "The Blind Fiancée"

Motif K1984.5: "Blind fiancée betrays self"

Informant: William Robert Glenn, May 6, 1972

Variants of this tale appear in Eastern Europe and in the United States in South Carolina, Missouri, Kentucky, Mississippi, Michigan, and Arkansas. In most of the tales an older, half-blind woman seeks a husband (sometimes younger). In Parsons's tale from the Sea islands ("Folklore of the Sea Islands, South Carolina," *Memoirs of the American Folklore Society* 16, no. 117 [1923]: 114) it is a one-legged woman; in Vance Randolph's tale from Missouri (*Who Blowed Up the Church House*, pp. 86–87, 206), it is a young, good-looking, half-blind girl; and in the Arkansas version (Julia Courtney, in Dorson's *American Negro Folktales*, pp. 336–38), it is a man who seeks a wealthy woman. A needle (cambric needle in South Carolina, darning needle in Kentucky) is planted in a gatepost (tree, gate) to be found later by the nearsighted woman to attest to her good eyesight. Food or drink is used in all the tales (except Parsons's variant from the Sea islands) as the object mistaken for the cat: coffee pot, pitcher of milk (buttermilk), black molasses pudding, turkey, chicken, and, in the Georgia tale, butter. Most of the variants use "Scat!" as the mistaken object is slapped off the table; a few indicate its feline identity by shouting "Tom!"

In Randolph's note in *Who Blowed Up the Church House* (p. 206) he indicates that his informant, A. W. Marshall, "heard this tale in southwest Missouri during the War between the States" and that "it is known all through the Ozark country."

The only tale that deviates radically in its ending is the South Carolina variant from the Sea islands. Here the old woman triumphs in convincing the young man of her hawklike vision only to be foiled by having him discover her one-legged condition on the wedding night. When he wants to leave, the old lady gives him a "box with five handles" for his fortune. In short, she kicks him five times and sends him away.

In the Bennett Cerf tale in *Laughing Stock,* the old woman is "a rich but well-seasoned old maid in Philadelphia" (cited in Jan Harold Brunvand, "Folktales by Mail from Bond, Kentucky," *Kentucky Folklore Record* 6 [1960]: 73–74). She fastens a diamond stick-pin onto a tree, but as she seeks to retrieve her jewelry, she trips over a cow.

17 · Anybody, Lord

Type 1476: "The Prayer for a Husband"

Motif J1811.1.1: "The old maid answers the owl's hoot, saying 'Anybody, Lord!' or giving the name of young man she wants." See also X750 "Jokes on Old Maids."

Informant: William Robert Glenn, May 6, 1972

Variants of this tale have been reported in Pennsylvania, New Jersey, New York, Texas, Indiana, and North Carolina. Most of the tales involve an old maid who wishes to marry so badly that she interprets the owl's "Who-o-o?" in light of her own dilemma and answers, "Anybody, Lord, just anybody." In Herbert Halpert's variant from Pennsylvania, however, his narrator, Leo Coddington, attributes the owl incident to his father, Jim Coddington ("Pennsylvania Fairylore and Folktales," *JAF* 58 [1945]: 133). When the owl hooted, "Who? Who?" the answer came, "Young Jim Coddington, b'God!" This tale was alluded to in William W. Rogers's history of Thomas County in regard to the need of more railway lines. "As one resident put it, 'Like the old maid's prayer, we are in a position to say: Any line, O, Lord' " (*Thomas County, 1865–1900* [Tallahassee: Florida State University Press, 1973], p. 123, as quoted in Thomasville *Times-Enterprise*, February 25, 1899).

18 · Good Grammar

Informant: William Robert Glenn, May 6, 1972

No exact parallel could be found for this tale; it does, however, incorporate motif K1984 "Girls keep up appearance to deceive suitors." For a tale in which improper language is used in a similar way see tale 22, "The Girls Who Could Not Talk Proper," in Portia Smiley, "Folklore from Virginia, South Carolina, Alabama, and Florida," *JAF* 32 (1919): 369.

19 · The Girl Who Ate So Little

Informant: William Robert Glenn, May 6, 1972

No exact parallel can be found for this tale. It shares kinship with type 1458 "The Girl Who Ate So Little" and incorporates motif K1984 "Girls keep up appearance to deceive suitors."

20 · How Big the Cook's Mouth

Informant: William Robert Glenn, May 6, 1972

Although no exact parallel could be found for this tale, it incorporates motif K1984 "Girls keep up appearance to deceive suitors." This same motif of deception was used in the television show "Maude" in 1978 during an episode in which Maude tells the story of the "Wide-Mouth Frog."

21 · Four Old Maids

Informant: William Robert Glenn, May 6, 1972

No parallel to this tale appears in either Thompson or Baughman. It falls generally under type 1475 "Jokes about Old Maids" and incorporates motif X750 "Jokes on old maids."

22 · Goat in the Pulpit

Type 1318A: "Robber or Animal in the Church Thought to Be a Ghost"

Motif J1782.1.2: "Sheep in abandoned church thought to be ghosts"

Informant: William Robert Glenn, May 6, 1972

The Grady County tale parallels many elements in the Arkansas variant as given in Vance Randolph's *Sticks in the Knapsack* (New York: Columbia University Press, 1958), p. 24: man seeks shelter in the old church on a rainy night, sees something white move, and after a bad fright realizes that the ghost is only an animal seeking shelter also. The revenant in the Georgia variant, however, is a goat, not a sheep.

23 · Frightened by Frogs

Motif J1811.5*(e): "Man in woods is scared by frogs. Little ones say, 'Get him!' The big ones say, 'Moderation!'"

Informant: William Robert Glenn, October 1974

The variant from North Carolina (Boggs, "White Folktales and Riddles," pp. 319–20), though very much like the Grady County tale in the cries of the frogs, is sparse in details compared to the Georgia variant. In the North Carolina tale, the interloper in the South is an Irishman; in the Georgia tale he is a salesman unacquainted with the noises of the country.

24 · Thief Reformed by Frogs

Motif J1811.5*(d): "Incorrigible thief hears frogs say, 'De-liver-up.' Reforms."

Informant: William Robert Glenn, October 1974

One variant of this tale is listed in Baughman—Richard Dorson's *Jonathan Draws the Long Bow* (Cambridge: Harvard University Press, 1946), pp. 18–19. Through imagination (or a guilty conscience) the thief in both tales becomes frightened and relinquishes the stolen item, which is a plug of tobacco in the Georgia tale. This story also reflects the love of chewing tobacco in the rural South, especially in the past.

25 · The Open Grave

Motif X828: "Drunk person falls in open grave with humorous results."

Informant: Allen Womble, August 17, 1972

Baughman lists only two states where variants of this tale have been reported: Kentucky and New Mexico. In two of the five versions from Kentucky and in the New Mexico variant, the interloper in the graveyard is drunk. Hence in three variants the humor is heightened by the retort of the drunk. New Mexico variant: Man riding by the grave says, "The meanest man in the world is lying there." Drunk in the grave replies, "You're a big liar. I am not the meanest man in the world." Roberts's Kentucky variant: Neighbors (hiding near grave to cure drunk by frightening him) say, "What are you doing in my grave?" Drunk says, "What the hell are you doing out of it?"[3]

In the other variants, a man falls into a grave at night, desperately tries to climb out, finally resigns himself to his entrapment, and huddles in the corner of the grave waiting for daylight. When the next unsuspecting fellow falls in, he goes through the same procedure, unaware of the presence of the first man. When the first man speaks (usually to say, "You can't get out"), the second man is so frightened he climbs right out of the grave and runs away.

Allen Womble, in his rendition of the Grady County version, interweaves the tale with factual happenings in the county and places himself in the role of the first man to fall into the hole. (For some time I was truly convinced that this was no tale but a memorate.) He places himself in a working situation—snaking logs with a team of animals—and locates his story near the sawmill. In fact, he and his friend Johnny Brown often cut through the graveyard on their way to the sawmill. Instead of a grave, Mr. Womble uses a large pit or a makeshift greenhouse (used by some Grady Countians in the past to store flowers for

3. Leonard Roberts, "Down Our Way: Unfinished Pages of Kentucky Folklore," *Kentucky Folklore Record* 1 (1955): 59; Dorothy J. Baylor, "Folklore from Socorro, New Mexico," Hoosier Folklore 6 (1947): 97.

the winter). This tale shows an excellent storyteller at work interlacing the bare framework of a story with graphic details of local history, thereby involving his audience totally and making his tale seem altogether believable.

26 · Ghost Scaring the Ghost

Type 1676A: "Big 'Fraid and Little 'Fraid"

Motif K1682.1: "Big 'Fraid and Little 'Fraid. Man decides to frighten another (or his son or servant). He dresses in a sheet; his pet monkey puts on a sheet and follows him. The person who is doing the scaring hears the victim say, "Run Big 'Fraid; Little 'Fraid'll get you.' The scarer sees the monkey in the sheet, runs home."

Informant: William Robert Glenn, October 1974

This tale where the would-be frightener is himself frightened has variants in many states—New Jersey, Illinois, Pennsylvania, Maryland, Alabama, Missouri, Texas, Virginia, North Carolina, South Carolina, Florida, Louisiana, and Kentucky. Grace Partridge Smith in her very convincing article on this tale ("The European Origin of an Illinois Tale," *Southern Folklore Quarterly* 6 [1942]: 89–94) concludes that the tale is of Old World origin and that it reached "America in the form of a local legend" (p. 93).

In most of the variants from the United States, the frightener is a father who is concerned about his son's laziness (or lateness) in driving the cows home. He therefore dons his ghost disguise (sheet) to frighten his son into greater industry. None of the European variants given by Smith use father, son, or cows, and none involve a monkey who imitates the frightener. (Most of the United States variants use the monkey as the second ghost.) The circumstances vary in her versions: a wife seeking to frighten her poet-magician husband, a shepherd wishing to frighten girls returning from breaking flax, a head-servant frightening a stableboy, a husband frightening his wife, the devil himself frightening a youth disguished as the devil.

The tale from Grady County also deviates from the norm in its beginning. Two plantation owners, concerned that their slaves are visiting more frequently between the plantations, determine to frighten them into remaining more at home. The two choose the site of an old gallows—about fifteen feet high—for the fright scene. No monkey is used in the tale, for the two men frighten each other.

Smith, in analyzing the various subtypes of the tale, deduces that the original form of this tale appeared as follows: The hero disguised as the devil receives a visit from the real devil. Hence, she maintains that the story "has undergone a process of progressive decay. The original is, of course, based on the widespread belief that by imitating or depicting evil spirits, one draws those spirits near" (p. 93). This ancient theme was subsequently levelled into the harmless prank seen in most of the United States variants.

27 · Fork in the Skirt

Type 1676B: "Clothing Caught in the Graveyard"

Motif N384.2(a): "Death in the graveyard; person's clothing is caught; the person thinks something awful is holding him; he dies of fright."

Informants: Version A, Athelone Barrett, March 21, 1976. Version B, Elmer Wilcox, August 3, 1976

The "Fork in the Skirt" tale with its widespread dissemination corroborates a statement made by L. A. Law in her article "Death and Burial Customs in Wiltshire," (*Folk-Lore* 11 [1900]: "One of the most common beliefs of the poor people in the fifties and sixties was the fear of the corpse, the dread of ghosts, and the unwillingness to enter graveyards at night" (p. 346). Repeatedly, as Herbert Halpert indicates, this tale is told as an actual occurrence, using such names as "Creek Yard Cemetery," "The old Hines place," or "Uncle Joe's grave." In most of the stories reported, the woman (boy, girl, soldier, priest, Betty Ream) is challenged to go into the graveyard (church, vault) to prove her or his bravery. When a reward is promised for this show of courage, it is usually money ($1.50–$10.00). For proof of this venture, the participant must drive a fork (stake, nail, stick, bayonet, shovel) into a grave (stump, altar). The object is mistakenly drawn into the participant's clothing, thereby creating the illusion that the corpse (evil spirit, ghost) has reached from the grave and snatched the intruder. The results are disastrous, bringing death by fright, or at least an all-night faint.

Three of the most different variants come from Wisconsin, Indiana, and Socorro, New Mexico. Richard Dorson, in his tale collected in Wisconsin, cites a modern adaption of the tale reported from Hanover, Germany, involving two soldiers. The soldier whittles in the graveyard awhile and then sticks his knife through his long cape ("Folklore at a Milwaukee Wedding," *Hoosier Folklore* 6 [1947]: 5). In the two variants from New Mexico the tale is given a religious rendering: version A involves a man who disbelieves that God is at the altar and who subsequently accepts the dare to drive a nail into the structure; version B revolves around a priest who, likewise, dares to walk into the church and hammer a nail into the wall (Dorothy Baylor, "Folklore from Socorro, New Mexico, Part 2," *Hoosier Folklore* 6 [1947]: 144). Halpert's Indiana variant, collected from Jim Pennington—regarded as one of the three best storytellers Halpert ever encountered—is rich with embellishment ("Indiana Storyteller," *Hoosier Folklore Bulletin* 1 [1942]: 58–59). The "Fork in the Skirt" motif becomes almost incidental in the lengthy account of an old lady (presumed to be a witch) and a beautiful young girl. The golden-haired girl eventually becomes engaged to a young man who ultimately begins to be plagued with all kinds of difficulties. Even the girl begins to mistrust the old woman. The old "haig" in time issues the fatal challenge to the young woman to place a fork in an unknown grave as a way of retrieving her fiancé.

Grace Partridge in "Notes as I Read" (*Hoosier Folklore* 6 [1947]: 107) maintains that the soldier in the graveyard is not solely German and cites additional references: "Dr. Bertram, *Sagen vom Ladogasee*, Helsinfors, 1872 (page reference not available); Marie Bonnet, 'Le Fuseau' in *Revue des traditions populaires* 27 (1912) 80ff; Otto Busch, *Nodwestthuringer Sagen* (Mulhausen, 1926) 32, 179; Charles Neely, *Tales and Songs of Southern Illinois* (Menasha, Wisc., 1938) 64–67. A story, 'The Cemetery Path,' appeared in the *Saturday Review of Literature*, November 29, 1941. In the literary version, Leonard Ross, the author, maintains that he read the story when he was nine or ten years old. The setting he gives is Russian, using the name "Ivan the Terrible" (derisively) for the victim, a young Cossack lieutenant as the challenger, and five gold rubles for the reward. The next morning Ivan is found dead in the cemetery with the lieutenant's saber stuck through the folds of his long coat. In later issues of this periodical, several persons reported the story—one from Argentina; two others, from Kentucky." For a Sicilian variant see J. Russell Reaver, "Fatalism in Sicilian Folktales," *Southern Folklore Quarterly* 35 (1971): 28.

One of the Grady County variants (told by Mrs. Barrett) has much similarity to those previously cited. In Mr. Wilcox's tale—although set

in Pisgah, a local cemetery—there is much deviation in the beginning
of the story. Here no dare is issued; no fork or other instrument is
involved. Rather, the protagonist (Mr. Butler) climbs atop a shelter
(used over a grave) to scare some young boys, his foot slips, the sheet is
hung on the shelter, and he faints from fright.

28 · Dividing the Souls

Type 1791: "The Sexton Carries the Parson"

Motif X424(a): "The Devil in the cemetery"

*Informants: Version A, William Robert Glenn, May 6, 1972. Version B,
Alto Sellers, September 11, 1975*

This tale, being one of the most popular and well-known anecdotes in
America and Europe, illustrates through its many variants the dynamic
aliveness of the folktale as it deletes, combines, and interchanges the
motifs through the years. Stith Thompson summarizes the two basic
forms of the tale: "In one there are sheep thieves [A sexton hears nuts
being cracked in the cemetery. Thinking it is the devil, he carries the
gouty parson on his back to where he encounters the thieves. The
thieves, thinking the duo are their comrade with a sheep, call out, "Is
he fat?" The frightened sexton drops the parson, shouting, "Fat or lean,
here he is!"] . . . . And in another there are merely boys dividing the
nuts" (*The Folktale*, pp. 213–14).

Hazel Harrod in 1949 brought together twenty-two variants of this
tale for analysis and traced the kernel of the story back to an A.D. 593
Latin tale (see "A Tale of Two Thieves," *Publications of the Texas
Folklore Society* 22 [1949]: 207–14). Although Harrod does not empha-
size the clerical involvement to any large degree, it is interesting to
note that in the Latin tale the power of the dead priest is so great that it
makes the sheep thief immobile as he passes the grave (see Charles H.
Beesom, *A Primer of Medieval Latin* [Chicago: Scott, Foresman and Co.,
1925], pp. 133–34). In subsequent tales which Harrod traces, the
churchman becomes less significant and even ludicrous. In her thir-
teenth-century French version the priest whose aid is sought is barefoot
and has to be carried to the site, only to flee in fear when he misunder-
stands the cabbage thief's threat (meant for the sheep) to slit his throat.
And in the fifteenth-century English version a representative from the
priest's house is the one carried and frightened. In thirty oral variants

assembled by Harrod and this author, only five involved a churchman. In the Missouri variant gathered by Vance Randolph the churchman or preacher is spoken of in quite derogatory terms. As he is "making too free with the womenfolks," two bear hunters lie in wait for him in the cemetery, one stating that he "don't mind killing preachers" (see Randolph, *Who Blowed up the Church House*, pp. 83–84).

Most of the earlier variants of the tale involve the sheep-thief motif. Later, Harrod maintains, the nut thief was added through a fifteenth-century variant (see *An Alphabet of Tales*, ed. Mary M. Banks [Paul Trench, Truber and Co., 1904], for the Early English Text Society, pp. 207–14). In this version there are two thieves. One is to steal a sheep; the other, nuts. Harrod points out that another new touch is also added here—the inclusion of the devil.

Although seven of the thirty variants accumulated (one each from Virginia and New York, two from Illinois, and three from North Carolina) incorporate the sheep thieves, the lame man carried on the shoulders, and the question "Is he fat or lean?" (excluding the nut motif), most of the variants simply have two people in the cemetery counting out nuts (fish, apples, oranges, jewelry, corn, shells). Seventeen of the tales incorporate the mistaken identity of the two as the devil and the Lord. These statistics only corroborate what Harrod summarized in her 1949 article: "The simple story with church characters and setting, a single sheep-thief, and a moral, expanded to a tale the crux of which was an amusing incident of mistaken identity rather than a serious moral and the characters of which included a nut thief and a sheep thief as well as a cleric. Gradually the church characters dropped out and only the graveyard setting remained: the sheep-tale finally became essentially a ghost-story. And in time it omitted the nut [thief] element, which then developed into a division-of-nuts-type-story having as its climax the same device as the sheep-thief tale—mistaken identity and misinterpretation of an ambiguous statement" (p. 284).

Two other items are of note. The churchman, who ultimately was used as a derisive figure, apparently was replaced predominately by the black man in the tale. (In two Canadian variants, as well as one variant from Grady County, the two Irishmen are used.) Elements of this tale were used, according to Elsie Clews Parsons, in the black musical comedy *Lisa* which played in New York around 1922 (see A. M. Bacon and Elsie Clews Parsons, "Folk-Lore from Elizabeth City County, Virginia," *JAF* 35 [1922]: 297).

The Grady County variant (A) is laced with details not found in other variants: detailed information on hickory nuts and their use and a description of graves in the preconcrete or marble days. In variant B the grave is covered with white shells which two Irishmen proceed to divide.

29 · What Did Paul Say?

Type 1833A: "Application of the Sermon"

Motif X435.1: "'What Says David?' The boy, 'Pay your old debt.'"

Informant: William Robert Glenn, October 29, 1974

This tale was in existence by the early sixteenth century and has been perpetuated through both oral and literary texts, such as *A C Mery Talys*. It has been reported in England, Canada, and at least fifteen states. In 1884 Mark Twain, along with four other authors, published the jest-book *Wit and Humor* (San Francisco: Law, King, and Law Publishing House, 1884), p. 348, which contained a variant of this tale. Roger Abrahams recorded a strikingly different variant in Philadelphia, one which is strewn with obscenities. The obscene language he attributes to verbal contests in which young blacks in the Camingerly group are expected to excell (*Deep-Down in the Jungle* [Chicago: Aldine Publishing Company, 1970], pp. 173ff.).

30 · Preacher's Rabbit

Type 1725: "Jokes about Parson"

New Motif GA X459.2(c): Boy hunts rabbit for preacher's dinner.

Informant: William Robert Glenn, May 6, 1972

Neither Stith Thompson nor Ernest Baughman lists this particular tale under the general categories about parsons. The motif given above suggests a new subdivision under X459 "Miscellaneous jokes about preachers." Entertaining the preacher, at least in southwest Georgia, was a big occasion, deserving of much good food and extensive preparation. Most rural families had chickens in the yard to be had for killing, plucking, cleaning, and eating. And to most preachers—so it was said repeatedly from the pulpit—nothing was more palatable than Southern

149

fried chicken. Some families, however, were so poor in this area that even chickens were beyond their means; hence, they had to resort to wild game if they had meat at all. Many people ate wild game, such as rabbits, coons, and possums, with relish; others, such as the preacher in this tale, found such fare less than desirable.

31 · "Let Gabriel Blow His Horn"

Type 1833J: "Preacher says: 'Let Gabriel Blow His Horn!' "

Motif X435.6: "Let Gabriel blow his horn—boy obliges." See also X411 "Parson put to flight during sermon."

Informant: Athelone Barrett, March 21, 1976

This church tale has known variants in Nova Scotia, New York, Pennsylvania, Kentucky, and Texas. The humor in most of these tales lies not so much in the show of fear by the congregation as in the cowardice of the preacher himself. In the Nova Scotia tale the preacher thinks that he has fallen into hell when he slips into a ditch during flight; a Philadelphia version shows him leaping through a window and catching his coattail on a hook (reminiscent of motif N384.2a "Death in the graveyard; person's clothing is caught"—here the Lord supposedly has him); in Dorson's Michigan tale the preacher is so frightened he not only runs over a hog but talks to him as well.[4] The tale suggests that preachers are often unaware of the verbiage they zealously fling at their audiences. When the preacher shouts for Gabriel to blow his horn, he is the very one most frightened when the horn actually blows.

The Grady County tale, like Leonard Roberts's Kentucky tale (in *South from Hell-fer-Sartin* [Lexington: University of Kentucky Press, 1955], p. 144), does not show the cowardice of the preacher but merely plays up the fright and flight of the black congregation. Here the jibe is aimed more at the fear of the blacks than at the minister.

4. Arthur H. Fauset, "Folklore from Nova Scotia," *Memoirs of the American Folkore Society* 24 (1931): 94; Arthur H. Fauset, "Tales and Riddles Collected in Philadelphia," *JAF* 41 (1928): 552; Richard M. Dorson, *American Negro Folktales* (Greenwich, Conn.: Fawcett Publications, 1967), p. 231.

32 · Possum in the Church

New Type GA 1838A: The Possum in the Church

Kinship with motif J1760: "Animal or person mistaken for something else"

Informants: Version A, Elmer Wilcox, August 3, 1976. Version B, Athelone Barrett, March 21, 1976

The new type number suggested above is a variation of 1838 "The Hog in the Church." There is no exact parallel to this tale given in Thompson or Baughman, although it falls under the general motif J1760 where mistaken identity is involved. Although in version B the possum is staged in the rafters of the church for a purpose, the other variant reflects a fairly common occurrence in south Georgia—animals straying into church services unasked (see introduction to the section on church-related humor).

33 · Mistletoe on the Preacher's Coattail

New Motif GA X459.1.4: Ousted minister asks congregation to take note of mistletoe attached to his coattail.

Informant: Elmer Wilcox, August 3, 1976

The above proposed motif falls under motif X459 "Miscellaneous jokes about preachers." There is no exact parallel in Thompson or Baughman. The preacher's anger is a result of the Baptist tradition of hiring and firing ministers at the whim of the deacons and membership.

34 · Jawbone of a Mule

New Motif GA X459.3: Preacher confuses scripture.

Informant: Elmer Wilcox, August 13, 1976

Having no parallel in Baughman or Thompson, this tale generally falls under X459 "Miscellaneous jokes about preachers."

Notes to the Tales

35 · The Nuns' Gasoline

New Motif GA X599.3: Jokes on nuns.

New Motif GA J1785.9: Gasoline mistaken for urine; bedpan used for container.

Informant: Elmer Wilcox, August 3, 1976

No exact parallels could be found in Baughman or Thompson. Motif GA X599.3 falls under the general division "Humor concerning other social classes"; the other falls under motif J1772 "One object thought to be another."

36 · Turned Out of Church

Informant: Elmer Wilcox, August 3, 1976

"Turned Out of Church" not only reflects the Primitive Baptists' weapon of excommunication but satirizes the hypocrisy of the system as well. Although no exact parallels are found in Baughman or Thompson, the tale suggests two motifs: J1260 "Repartee based on church or clergy" and J1262 "Repartee based on doctrinal discussions."

37 · Corpse Sits Up in Coffin

Informant: Elmer Wilcox, August 3, 1976

William L. Montell in *Ghosts Along the Cumberland* (Knoxville: University of Tennessee Press, 1975), pp. 202–3, lists four Kentucky variants of motif J1769.2 "Dead man thought to be alive." In all four variants the corpse sits up in the coffin; variant D, however, is closer to the Grady County variant with the deformed corpse, the instructions to "lay back down," and the reference to keeping the cats off the corpse.

38 · The Giant Bedbug

Informant: Leroy Mann, August 15, 1972

No close parallel is listed in Baughman or Thompson; several motifs, however, are incorporated: X1291 "Lies about bedbugs" and X1291(a) "Large bedbugs." For a motif showing some kinship see J1772.1.1 "Boy thinks terrapin hatches from bedbug eggs." Leonard Roberts in *South from Hell-fer-Sartin* gives a variant that is quite similar to the Grady County tale; he suggests Motif X1021.8* "The great bedbug" (pp. 150–51, 263).

This tale revolves around a contest in lying, whether it be competition between the New Englander and the Texan or between the Englishman and the American. In most of the variants a turtle or terrapin is mistaken for a bedbug; occasionally a lobster is used.

39 · Is the Corn Shucked?

Type 1951: "Is Wood Split?"

Motif W111.5.10.1: "Lazy man is being taken to poorhouse or to cemetery to be buried alive."

Informant: William Robert Glenn, December 2, 1979

This tale, although found predominately in the northeastern United States, has also been reported as far south as South Carolina, Texas, and now Georgia. The tale from Grady County, however, is almost identical to some of the variants in the Northeast: New Jersey, New York, Philadelphia.

Richard Dorson in *Jonathan Draws the Long Bow* states that "folktales of the insuperably lazy Yankee fill native humor. Commonest is the starving idler who, proffered a bushel of corn, asks, 'Is it shelled?' " (p. 253). This same motif is reflected in some of the New England ballads cited by Dorson, and it, likewise, is seen in proverbial lore as given by Harold W. Thompson, in *Body, Boots and Britches* (New York: N. B. Lippincott Co., 1940), p. 486. New York state has a proverb about a lazy man which, Thompson points out, conceals a folktale: "He wants his corn shelled" (pp. 485–86). The tale Thompson cites is almost identical with the Georgia variant. This tale has made its way into three different genres of folklore—the folktale, the ballad, and the proverb.

40 · Worms in the Mouth

Informant: William Robert Glenn, May 6, 1972

There are motifs designated by Baughman for lies about tobacco chewing and spitting (see X933a and X934) but none about the exaggerated love of tobacco itself. No variants have been found by this author for the Grady County tale. This inordinate love of chewing tobacco in the tale, however, is reflective of its importance in the lives of rural males in the early part of this century. Mr. M. P. Maxwell, a longtime resident in the county, maintains that "most men and boys regarded chewing tobacco and 'Spit Red' as a sort of coming-up thing that showed you were no child any longer" (interview, August 13, 1972).

41 · Ten Hens and a Rooster with One Shot

New Motif GA X1124.3.2: Lie: accidental discharge of gun kills ten hens and a rooster.

Informant: Elmer Wilcox, August 3, 1976

This tale, although having no exact parallel in Baughman or Thompson, falls under the general motif X1122.2 "Lie: person shoots many animals with one shot." The tale might fall under type 1890 "The Lucky Shot" except the man in the Grady County variant is trying to protect his chickens, not kill them. Baughman, however, does add a note under type 1890: "The accidental discharge of the gun is not a characteristic motif of the English nor of the American forms of the type. In each variant, the weapon is used deliberately, although luckily" (*Type and Motif Index*, p. 54).

J. Russell Reaver alludes to a related variant of this tale, motif X1110 "The wonderful hunt," in his analysis of its narrative movement (see "From Reality to Fantasy: Opening-Closing Formulas in the Structure of American Tall Tales," *Southern Folklore Quarterly* 36 [1972]: 371–72). The Grady County variant, however, shows no vertical development beyond the initial accidental shot which kills the fowl.

42 · The Coon-Monkey

New Motif GA X1232*(b): Monkey trained to kill raccoons with a gun.

Informant: Allen Womble, August 17, 1972

Several motifs are contained in this tall tale (X1232 "Lies about monkeys" and X1124 "Lie: the hunter catches or kills game by ingenious or unorthodox method") although no parallels are found in

Baughman or Thompson. The tale also has elements which share kinship with motifs X1211(bb) "Cats hunt 'coons'" and X1215.8(a) "Intelligent hunting dog." Inherent in the tale is the great enjoyment of "coon hunting," a favorite sport of many Grady County males in the past. Only a few still participate in the sport and keep hounds today.

43 · Underground Woodpecker

New Motif GA X1269*(b): Large woodpecker flies out of log which is un-covered while digging a well.

Informant: M. P. Maxwell, August 13, 1972

Neither Baughman nor Thompson lists a parallel to this tale; it does incorporate the general motif X1269 "Lies about woodpeckers." This tale, like "The Hard Rain," supposedly came from a bearer of tall tales named George, a member of a road-working detail.

44 · The Hard Rain

Motif X1654.3.1*(a): "In hard rain, the rain goes into the bunghole of barrel faster than it can run out both ends." See also X1611.1.13.6*(a) "Sand goes through bunghole of barrel faster than it can run out of both ends."

Informant: M. P. Maxwell, August 13, 1972

Baughman lists four variants of this tale: two in general collections of folktales and two from New York and Indiana. The allusion to the heavy rain in the variants is usually placed in a local setting to give verity to the tale. In the Grady County variant Mr. Maxwell places the setting near Ochlocknee, Georgia (about fifteen miles from Cairo). A series of tall tales were told by a man named George, a local citizen assisting with road work in the early part of this century.

45 · Mule Almost Drowns in Mud-hole

New Motif GA X1655.2*(e): Mud-hole so deep that mule almost drowns

Informant: M. P. Maxwell, August 3, 1972

Since no parallels to this tale could be found in Thompson or Baugh-man, a new motif subdivision is in order, falling under the more general classification X1655.2* "Deep mud." This tale Mr. Maxwell also attributes to George, whose lies entertained the road-working detail in Mr. Maxwell's time. This tale alludes to the tradition of traveling to the coast in a wagon for salt fish.

46 · Suicide Attempt with Carbolic Acid

New Motif GA X1739.2: Man swallows carbolic acid.

Informant: Elmer Wilcox, August 3, 1976

This tall tale includes numerous motifs (X1723 "Lies about swallowing," X1731 "Lies about falling," and X1740 "Absurd disregard of natural laws") although no exact parallel is given in Baughman or Thompson. The many motifs are themselves suggestive of a tale built upon "perpendicular lying" as its manner of narrative movement (see Reaver, "From Reality to Fantasy, headnote for tale 41). The narrator here builds one fantastic happening upon another. Hence, Reaver suggests, "this intensity through repetition creates the distinctive world of fantasy that is the artistic and psychological aim of the popular tall tale" (p. 372).

47 · Nothing Except the Fence

Motif J1649(e): "Person asks native where the road goes. Reply: 'No place.'"

Informant: William Robert Glenn, May 6, 1972

The repartee in this tale is part of "The Arkansas Traveler" sequence. The variant from New Jersey (see Herbert Halpert, "Folktales and Legends from the New Jersey Pines," pp. 423 and 665) is almost identical in dialogue to the one from Grady County. Catherine M. Vineyard in her article "The Arkansas Traveler" (*Publications of the Texas Folklore Society* 16 [1943]: 11) described this sequence: "The dialogue as we know it today is a collection of themes of folk wit and humor, many of which can be found in other stories and some of which can be traced through centuries of folklore." The sequence has been perpetrated through song, verse, and drama as well as through oral tradition.

48 · Sheephead and Dumplings

Motif J1813.8: "Sheep's head has eaten dumplings. Small boy is at home to watch the dinner while mother (or master) is in church. He runs into church, calls out to her that the sheep's head has eaten all the dumplings (or butted them out of the pot)."

Informant: William Robert Glenn, May 6, 1972

Herbert Halpert in "Folktales and Legends from the New Jersey Pines" lists eleven variants of this tale, distributed in Texas, Illinois, Virgin Islands, Antilles, Newfoundland, Norfolk, Cambridge, Derby, and Cornwall. The tale is also found in Cornwall Wright's *The Jests of Scogin*, in *Shakespeare's Jest-Books* 2:60–61, and in Joel C. Harris, *The Complete Tales of Uncle Remus*, compiled by Richard Chase (Boston: Houghton Mifflin Co., 1955), pp. 719–20. This tale in the Harris story is entitled "The Hard-Headed Woman." Names of the boy vary, some tales using Jack, John, or even Andreahs (from the Virgin Islands). In most of the tales accumulated it is the mother who leaves a boy (usually her son) to look after the boiling pot. In the Dorson tale from *American Negro Folktales* it is Old Marster. Most of the tales incorporate the sheephead and dumplings with variations, such as hoghead and peas (Dorson), calamus root (Harris story), and a calf's head (New Jersey, in Halpert, "Folktales and Legends from the New Jersey Pines," pp. 407–8, 653). The final lines of the variants to this story are very similar to the one here from Grady County. Exceptions: "That hoghead done ate all those peas and got his mouth open trying to catch them two or three bubbling round the top" (Dorson); and "sh sh be damned. . . . The sheep's head has ett all the taters an' the apple dumpling has took off his jacket to fight it" (Bales, "Folklore from West Norfolk," *Folklore* 50 [1939]: 73). The tale having the greatest variance is Florence O. Meade's tale collected from the Virgin Islands. The son Andreahs steals a dumpling, puts it in his bosom, and shouts to his "Aunti Noni" that a scorpion has stung him. It is the quicksilver which is thrown into the pot which causes the dumplings to jump out. The mother then whips Andreahs; the sheephead begins to upbraid her, saying, "You are an old fool to put me to boil with horns," and promptly gives her three good butts which send her rolling. In the Uncle Remus tale the water in the pot, prior to receiving the sheephead and dumplings, is laced with gourd-vine flower, thunderwood buds, and calamus root. The hitherto enduring husband of the hardheaded woman, through adding these ingredients, spitting in the ashes, making a cross-mark, and turning around twice, seeks to retaliate against his shrew. Hence, at the appropriate time, the pot begins to boil, 'an' de peas, dey flew'd out an' rattled on de' flo' like a bag er bullets done busted" ("Folk Tales from the Virgin Islands," *JAF* 15 [1932]: 365–66).

The Grady County tale places the setting in "the old horse-and-buggy days" with a "widow woman" and her son. There is more detailed description of the stove and the fire than in the other variants, using such wording as "old wooden stove" and "fatwood." The "fatwood," of course, causes the pot to boil over, spilling the dumplings on the floor. The preacher also receives distinctive description in this tale, with the informant's calling him "one of these long-winded, pot-liquor preachers."

49 · The Obstinate Wife

Type 1365B: "Cutting with the Knife or the Scissors"

Motif T255.1: "The obstinate wife, cutting with knife or scissors"

Informant: William Robert Glenn, October 29, 1974.

Variants of this tale have been reported in England, Canada, and in various places in the United States—New Jersey, New York, Wisconsin, Indiana, Vermont, and North Carolina. In all of the variants, a couple (a man and a woman) are arguing. The cause of the argument varies: how their boat was cut adrift (West Norfolk), whether to call a certain implement tongs or scissors (Wisconsin), whether the color of a horse is black or white (Alberta). In the New York version the shrewish wife plagues her tailor husband by calling him "Scissors." And in both the North Carolina and Georgia versions the quarrelsome wife is simply nagging her husband for a pair of scissors.[5] Becoming increasingly furious with his spouse, the man, in most versions, pushes her into a river (pond, millpond, creek). As she goes down for the last time, she

---

5. E. G. Bales, "Folklore from West Norfolk," *Folk-Lore* 50 (1939): 73; Charles E. Brown, "Wisconsin Versions of 'Scissors,'" *Hoosier Folklore Bulletin* 2 (1943): 46–47; Herbert Halpert, "Tall Tales and Other Yarns from Calgary, Alberta," *California Folklore Quarterly* 4 (1945): 48; Halpert, "Folktale and 'Wellerism'—a Note," *Southern Folklore Quarterly* 7 (1943): 75; Boggs, "North Carolina White Folktales and Riddles," p. 306.

makes the sign of the scissors with her fingers. Only in one variant (Wisconsin, version 2) is this humorous tale burdened with any guilt or remorse on the part of the husband, and he subsequently hangs himself. All tales, however, end with the obstinate's wife's getting the last word. One of the Wisconsin versions (no. 1) has a delightful ending which further attests to the wife's obstinacy. After she drowns in the millpond, the narrator says that "even the water in the race flowed backward." Of much interest also is Herbert Halpert's note on this story in "Folktale and 'Wellerism,'" *Southern Folklore Quarterly* 7 (1943): 75. Halpert has evidence that this tale, through reduction, has been used as a kind of proverbial phrase—a "Wellerism." In short, in a heated argument a woman might just walk away, showing the sign of the scissors and repeating the phrase, "Well, as the old woman said as he pushed her under the water . . ."

Richard Dorson in *Jonathan Draws the Long Bow* (Cambridge: Harvard University Press, 1946), pp. 230–31, suggests that "The Obstinate Wife" is quite comparable to a story that Rowland E. Robinson uses in *Uncle Lisha's Shop* (pp. 139, 159). Dorson's variant comes from the *Yankee Blade* 13 (December 17, 1853).

50 · Bundle of Twigs

Type 910F: "The Quarreling Sons and the Bundle of Twigs. Peasant puts twigs together and cannot break them. Separately they are easily broken. His sons apply the lesson."

Informant: Allie Ben Prince, July 1972 (version A)

This tale like so many others in the collection shares both a literary and an oral tradition. The heritage of this tale is an old one, going back as far as the fables of Aesop or earlier. Joseph Jacobs includes the tale in his 1906 edition of *The Fables of Aesop* (New York: Macmillan Co.), p. 173, and states in his notes that "a similar apologue is told of Ghenghis Khan and occurs in Harkon's *Armenian History of the Tartars*. Plutarch tells it of a King of Scythia (*Apophth.* 84, 16)" (p. 217).

Interestingly enough, a version of this tale appeared in the Grady County newspaper, the *Cairo Messenger* (August 14, 1908). In this more modern version of the tale (see version B), the son, unlike the son in the Aesop tale, does not think very highly of his father's moralistic parable on the principles of business.

Appendix 1 · The Dumb-bull

Different stories abound in the local area about one item of material culture—the dumb-bull—which was still in existence in the early part of this century. It was notorious primarily as a prankster's tool or toy, yet it could be used to achieve more serious results, such as ridding a neighborhood of undesirables. The dumb-bull was a device that emitted a harrowing, hair-raising roar reminiscent of a wild bull, a lion, a panther, or some ungodly monster. The roar was so effective that it could be heard for two or three miles on a quiet night and could cause livestock to break out of stalls and stampede. There is even a case where its effect was so devastating to a human being that it supposedly almost caused his death. Several Grady Countians maintain that a city ordinance finally had to be passed outlawing the use of the dumb-bull.

The construction of the dumb-bull was relatively simple but could be handled in several ways, according to longtime residents in the county. The directions given by Mr. Allen Womble describe two different methods of construction:

> You take a piece of goat-hide or cowhide, soak it in water till it's good and pliable, then stretch it tight over part of a stovepipe, a keg, or even a section of a hollow black-gum tree. After you stretch the hide in place, tie it real tight onto your keg or whatever you're using. It looks like a drum by the time you get this done. You then put a hole in the middle of it, pull a good strong cord (about three feet long) through, knot the end of your cord so that it doesn't come through, and finally rub your cord real good with beeswax or rosin. The noise comes from the way you slide your fingers over that string which has been pulled tight. There are more tricks to that rosin string than you would think. In fact, you could create almost the same effect with wood shingles. You know when they used to roof houses with wood shingles, you could go up on the roof, drive a tack in the shingle, tie your string around that nail, and rub the string with rosin. When you slide your fingers over that string, almost every board on that house would rattle. (Interview, August 17, 1972)

Mr. Robert Glenn, however, maintains that the hollow log is far superior to any other type of material for the construction of the dumb-bull:

Well, you got to find a hollow tree just right, and they're pretty hard to find. However, you can use a can about the size of a gallon syrup can; half a gallon would also do fairly well. But wouldn't anything come up to a hollow tree. You have to take a hollow tree about two feet long and hollow it out thin. Most of them is too thick; you have to keep hollowing it to get it out thin. The diameter is six, eight, maybe ten inches. Oh, if it was twelve inches, it would be all right. They used to take a goat-hide or a cowhide that was dried—they used to keep a lot of them around to make shoestrings and all kinds of things like that. Coonhide would be all right. They'd soak it in water, and then they'd stretch it tight over one end of that hollow gum. The gum makes the best one, 'cause it don't split very easily. Then they could put a little bitty hole right in the center and take a long cord—good cord. They'd tie a stick crossways on one end of the cord, so it couldn't slip through that hole, and that stick would keep it from going through. Then they would take beeswax and wax that cord good. And after they waxed it good, then you could put that cord between your fingers and just let it slip—pull like this—and, great goodness, it would wake up the dead. (Interview, October 17, 1974)

Still another type of construction is given by Gordon Wilson in his article "Mammoth Cave Words—More Neighborhood Doings" where he defines "dumb-bull" according to Kentuckians as "a noise-making contrivance made by attaching a fishing line to a nail in the bottom of a lard stand; a fishhook is attached to the other end of the string. When the hook is fastened to a window sash and a wad of *rozum* is rubbed on the taut string, enough noise to wake the dead is produced. Other names for this invention is *rozum the string, squeegie, horse fiddle, or tick-tack.*"[1]

The storytelling tradition which has been built up through the years is predominantly centered around three functions of the dumb-bull: to play pranks on friends (enemies, rivals); to reform the lazy, shiftless, and irresponsible person through fright; and to rid the neighborhood of undesirables.

The dumb-bull is probably most notorious in its function as the prankster's toy. Although pranks are not unique to Grady County, they certainly were still very much in vogue in the pretelevision days when the principal entertainment consisted of social gatherings, radio programs, or an occasional movie on Saturday. To many, the best pranks were the roughest ones where the scapegoat was sometimes the black person or the mentally retarded—anyone who was deemed by the prankster to be susceptible to superstitious beliefs or incapable of discerning that a prank was in process. The following two tales told by Mr.

1. *Kentucky Folklore Record* 11 (1965): 78.

The Dumb-bull

Allen Womble form a portion of the prankster tradition built around the dumb-bull.

The Scaring of Johnny Quick

Johnny Quick, who was a mighty scary man, would pass the cemetery every day on his way home. Well, some of the Harrison boys decided that this was too good to resist, so they decided they'd scare Johnny. Now, it was time for Johnny to come along this particular evening; in fact, it was just about first dark.

One of the Harrison boys appeared from the doorway of the church with a sheet draped over him; another one came from out of the grave-yard, waving his arms under a white sheet; and the other one was stationed down the road a piece with a dumb-bull. Johnny saw the one in the cemetery first, then spied the one in the churchyard. By this time he was already running down the road, but when he passed the third Harrison boy and heard that dumb-bull, he knew that he was gotten for sure. Well, he put himself into about tenth gear and ran for his life all the way home.

When he got home, he almost went through the front door, he was in such a state of shock. When he ran up on the front porch and hit the front door, his mama, who was a widow lady, came running out to find Johnny lying there in a cold sweat, just like you'd thrown a bucket of water on him. She saw that he was in bad shape and barely breathing. So she ran up to Preacher Sellers's house and said, "There's something wrong with Johnny. Come quick!"

When they went down to see him, they found the fellow nearly dead. They finally got him into a buggy and got him to the doctor, but it was a week or more before they could get him on his feet again. It was not long after this that the dumb-bull was outlawed around here. In fact, they would not put you in the jail if they caught you with one; they'd put you under it.

The Scaring of Barwick and Bradshaw

This old man, Barwick, was going to see an old maiden girl, the Crutchfield girl, who lived up the road there in the Maxwells' community.

163

He'd set with her at her house until ten or eleven o'clock; then he would go home. There was a little branch head [spring] down there. He'd always get him a song a-going, or whistle to scare the boogers off. So that's what the Maxwells figured, that he'd make a lot of noise so the boogers wouldn't get him. He was kind of jumpy. So Morris Maxwell and some of the other fellows in the community—I think it was Morris they told it on—had made them a dumb-bull.

Well, they go down to this branch head, and here comes Barwick whistling. He was just whistling. The Maxwells were ready for him. The tighter you hold the line on the dumb-bull and the slower you pull it, the rougher he growls. You can make it change its tone by gripping the string. So Morris just growled on it. Sounded like some kind of monster. Barwick's whistling hushed, so Morris didn't make any more noise until Barwick had passed. He growled it out again, real loud, not knowing that right around the corner of a lot of land on another settlement road the way Barwick was going there was a Negro man that had been to see his girl friend, too. And his name was Jack Bradshaw. And Jack said, "Now, what was that I heard?"

Jack said, "Mr. Bryant"—he was later telling Mr. Bryant about this—"now, I can run, and I know I can run. I can move on out the country. I heard it the first time, but I thought it was a cow or something; I didn't pay no attention. But the next time, I could tell it was a big cat or something another down in that swamp. And it sounded like it was right over there."

He said in three or five minutes he really was lots closer and really sounded off then. He said, "Then's when I was doing about full speed going down that settlement road. I just kicked like that, you know, and I run by and reached out and got that shoe. I kicked that foot, and I run by, and I got that other shoe and I was going. Now, I ought to have been home already. I was going in home. Then's when it happened. I heard him coming up behind me. I knowed he was gonna git me. He was gitting closer and closer. I had done put both shoes in one hand, reached up and got my hat. Then I was running at full speed. And like I told you, Mr. Bryant, I know I can go. I was going. I was done leaning on them curves like I was riding a motorcycle. Just about the time I knowed this thing was a-gitting me, up pulled Mr. Barwick. I don't think either one of us stopped to speak to the other one. We just kept on running till we reached our own houses.

The following two stories describe further use of the dumb-bull as an instrument of fright. The first was collected from Mr. G. B. Trulock (interview,

The Dumb-bull

June 17, 1976); the second, from Mr. Elmer Wilcox (interview, August 3, 1976).

Scare at the Bank

I never did make but one. At the bank here in Whigham then, they had the heavy, heavy wire screen on the back window as a guard. So, I got a string—a long string, maybe a hundred feet long—and fastened it to that steel screen, and I believe I had a lard can lid or something on the other end. And I took a piece of rosin and just scraped that, and I would make an ungodly noise. So, we had the cashier at the bank working late one night—that was in 1915, I believe—and I decided I would frighten him.

He was up there at the desk working, and I rigged me up one and give it two or three yanks there with my rosin. He raised up—I had to watch him—and did an unexpected thing. He got up and went around front and came out with a pistol and shot three times right at the back door.

Scaring of the Butlers

They said they had this Mrs. Butler, and her husband was real scary. And they said somebody was off out there pulling on that rosin. She said, "Get up, John, go see about it; somebody's trying to tear in." No, he wouldn't get up. And they used these long old splinters—those fat lightered splinters—and she got up and lit those splinters, walking around the house. And she burnt the string in two, so that cut out the noise. But they were scared to go back up to the house.

Mr. Alto Sellers tells one story where the dumb-bull was used on a lazy farmhand:

> Mr. Banks, he was just in a bad fix; he couldn't get about too good. And they tell me that there was one fellow back there in the corner of that field got to hitching his mule, then taking off to go fishing. And Mr. Banks got to watching him, and he seen him take off. He got down there, got to looking, and he got his dumb-bull. And he went to playing that thing, and that fellow come out of there like a whirlwind. When he got out, his mule had got so scared till he went right through the field with his plow, plowing it right up. And I said to myself, "Well, my lands, he ought

165

to have been scared, to quit plowing and go fishing." (Interview, September 11, 1975)

Mr. Elmer Wilcox corroborates the view that the dumb-bull was used in a more serious way—to remove undesirables from a neighborhood.

People back then, if they didn't like somebody in the neighborhood, they'd try to run them out. They didn't have the law to come in and take them all out, so they'd get them up a bunch of men and torture them awhile. Then they could take a piece of timber and hew it out hollow, and then they'd take some kind of skin from animals, and they'd put it in the creek—they call that tanning, what they do to it now. They'd stretch that thing over that barrel and put a string through it and put rosin on it. It made the awfullest noise you ever heard in your life. They called it the dumb-bull. . . .

They had some black folks; you know they didn't want black folks living close to you back then. So they was going to scare those folks with it, and they did. They moved out in about a night or two. They'd go over there in the daytime and tell them there was a panther loose—to be on the watch for him. Then they'd get out the dumb-bull that night. The black folks would think that panther was coming.[2]

The dumb-bull, while tales of it abound in the southern region of the United States, possibly shares a much broader heritage. The description of its construction calls to mind an early musical instrument called a "friction drum." Curt Sachs, in his book *The History of Musical Instruments*, gives the following description of such an instrument: "Most friction drums have either a friction cord or a friction stick. The cord passes through a center hole in the membrane. . . . In most cases the skin is set into vibration when the stick or cord is rubbed with resinous fingers."[3]

Sachs maintains that although the friction drum looks very much like the struck drum, it differs considerably in the way it is played and is hence probably associated with tribal ceremonies. "As the rubbing action with its to-and-fro movement symbolizes cohabitation, the friction drum is the characteristic instrument at boys' and girls' initiations in Africa" (p. 40). The latest descendant of the friction drum is, according to Sachs, the "whirled friction drum" which is a toy found in Africa, Asia, Europe, and the United States. Unlike its ancestor, the friction

2. Interview, August 3, 1976. For another story involving the dumb-bull mistaken for a panther see Vance Raldolph, *The Devil's Pretty Daughter* (New York: Columbia University Press, 1955), pp. 42–44, 180–81.

3. *The History of Musical Instruments* (New York: W. W. Norton and Co., 1940), p. 39.

drum, the whirled friction drum is suspended from a small rod by its cord. When the drum is whirled, the vibrations of the cord are sent to the pasteboard membrane. Sachs's last statement on this toy suggests a kinship with the Australian "bull-roarer": "Its whirled friction drum, Dutch name, *ronker*, or "snorer," is descriptive of its sound; the German name, *Waldteufel*, or "forest-devil," is probably reminiscent of ancient rites in which the friction drum may have produced a demon's voice, like the *bull-roarer*, of which it may possibly be a descendent on account of its being whirled" (p. 40).

If the dumb-bull is indeed a descendant of the friction drum, and I do maintain that it is, then it is very likely that its heritage is linked to a bull-roarer which is still significant in tribal rituals of Australia and New Guinea. In the *Standard Dictionary of Folklore, Mythology, and Legend*, the bull-roarer is defined as "a flat oval slab of bone, stone, or wood, tapered toward each end, with a cord or thong threaded through a hole near one end, by which it is whirled over the head to produce a harsh roaring or wailing sound. The magic symbolism of the bull-roarer derives partly from its shape and decoration, partly from its weird and terrifying sound, partly from the variations in size of the instruments."[4]

The bull-roarer, when it is used in Australia or New Guinea, is usually an accompaniment to puberty and initiation rites of young boys. Although procedures vary from tribe to tribe, the pattern is generally the same: young boys are led into the forest away from the village where their circumcision and, frequently, subincision take place after a period of deprivation and hardships. Bull-roarers are swung by men hidden away to test the young men's courage and to symbolize spirits or monsters who must figuratively bear the boy away to make room for the man who will emerge after the ordeal. Women and the uninitiated are forbidden at these ceremonies.

The function of the bull-roarer has changed considerably in transmission from culture to culture. In the Malay Peninsula it has descended to the practical function of scaring elephants away from plantations. It is interesting to speculate that in Grady County of the early 1900s the dumb-bull was possibly a descendent of the bull-roarer of aboriginal tribes, though its function here primarily was to entertain. Even if the dumb-bull's heritage cannot be substantiated with formal proof, this small item of material culture is a reminder of the common bonds which unite past with present and link us undeniably with people of other lands.

4. Maria Leach, ed., Standard *Dictionary of Folklore, Mythology, and Legend* (New York: Funk and Wagnalls Co., 1949), 2:170.

Appendix 2 · The Oral Style of Two Narrators

Dan Ben-Amos in "Toward a Definition of Folklore in Context" stresses the importance of folklore as a communication process; in particular he would eliminate the hiatus that has existed between narrators and their tales. "There is dichotomy," he maintains, "between processes and products. The telling is the tale; therefore, the narrator, his story, and his audience are all related to each other as components of a single continuum which is the communicative event."[1]

This chapter seeks to look at the art of storytelling in such a continuum through focusing upon two outstanding narrators in this collection, Mr. Robert Glenn and Mr. Allen Womble. Three focuses form the basis for this analysis: the repertory of tales possessed by each narrator, the creative role of the storyteller in relation to his audience, and the stylistic devices of the gifted raconteur.

Each of these narrators has his own repertory, his own collection of stories which seem to belong to him. "The born raconteur," wrote Linda Dégh, "quite conscious of the fact that the fate of the story is determined by him alone, regards it as his or her own mental product, whereas storytellers of a more inferior category do not feel as the owners of the tales."[2] The repertory of Mr. Robert Glenn, although it includes both long and short narratives, seems to concentrate on the brief, punch-endings jest, as Richard Dorson calls one of his selections of content.[3] There are supernatural tales and humorous tales primarily built around the church, Irishmen, relationships between the sexes, and farming. Mr. Womble specializes in the long, heavily detailed narrative, and although he tells both supernatural and humorous tales, he has a larger assortment

1. Dan Ben-Amos, "Toward a Definition of Folklore in Context," JAF 84 (1971): 5.
2. Linda Dégh, "Some Questions of the Social Functions of Storytelling," Acta Ethnographica 6 (1957–58): 134.
3. Richard M. Dorson, "Oral Styles of American Folk Narrators," in Folklore: Selected Essays (Bloomington: Indiana University Press, 1972), p. 105.

of the former, especially witch tales. Both narrators tend to compare with what Mark Azadovsky, the Russian folklorist, describes as the second type of storyteller: "For him the exact repetition of the story and all its details is of great importance. He tells everything without hurry, at the same time elaborating every detail and taking care with the proper effect to be produced."[4]

Mr. Womble said, "There are some people who can tell a story, and there's nothing to it. Then there are others who tell a joke, and Lord-a-mercy, you just bust your sides a-laughing, and the more you think about it the funnier it gets." And when Irene Womble, who formed part of the audience for the tale-telling, admonished him, saying, "Allen, they don't want to hear all that part about what you thought at the moment," he retorted, "You want me to hit just the high places and miss all what makes a story good." Just what does make a story good? What constitutes the difference between those who merely relate the bare outline of the story and the real storyteller?

William Jansen in his article "Classifying Performance in the Study of Verbal Folklore" emphasized the need for more awareness of the narrator's actual performance, for "the speaker steps outside himself as an individual and assumes a pose toward his audience"—either of the teacher, the monitor, or the entertainer.[5] In either case, the narrator plays to his audience, altering his story as necessary to fit the occasion, time, and place. The whole process is a creative one, for the narrator must, as Richard Dorson says, "select, arrange, describe, connect the parts" (p. 114). And J. L. Fischer, in his article "The Sociopsychological Analysis of Folktales," discusses the narrator's assumption of the creative role: "The storyteller learns his story and tells it only in a social situation. As he tells it, he perceives numerous subtle cues—and some not so subtle—from his audience, broadly indicating their approval or disapproval of each segment of his narration. Even if he conceives it his duty to reproduce the tale verbatim, he can hardly help making cumulative small emendations in many tellings if audience pressure demands them."[6]

A story recorded from Robert Glenn on two different occasions cor-

4. Mark Azadovsky, *Eine Sibirische Märchenerzählerin*, quoted in Stith Thompson, *The Folktale* (New York: Dryden Press, 1946), p. 452.

5. William Hugh Jansen, "Classifying Performance in the Study of Verbal Folklore," in *Studies in Folklore*, ed. W. Edson Richmond (Bloomington: Indiana University Press, 1957), p. 113.

6. J. L. Fischer, "The Sociopsychological Analysis of Folktales," *Current Anthropology* 4 (1963): 237.

roborates the subtle changes made by a narrator because of audience. The tale is one entitled "Nothing Except the Fence" (tale 47). The first recording of this tale was made May 6, 1972, when the audience consisted of three adults and two children, the latter whose approximate ages were ten and twelve years old. Almost two years later, on October 29, 1974, the same tale was recorded again, but this time only two adults and no children were present.

Version A

This happened years ago. Back then, people in the community, especially farmers, were poor, and they were working a crop on shares—well, we call it on halves—for the landowners. One little boy he was out plowing the corn aside of the fence, and the corn did look mighty bad; they didn't use much fertilizer. This traveling salesman came by in a horse-drawn buggy, and since he wadn't in a hurry, he just decided he'd stop and talk to the boy a little bit. He said, 'Whoa, Maude!" and the horse stopped. The little boy's plowing out to the end, and the salesman said, "Well, howdy, son."

The boy said, "Howdy do, sir?"

So the salesman said, "Well, I was just passing by and decided I'd stop and talk with you a little bit."

The little boy said, "Well, I'm glad you did. I'm a little tired myself, and I need a rest here."

"Son, just looking at your corn, it looks mighty yellow."

"Yes sir, we planted the yellow kind."

"Well, son, I don't believe you gonna make no more than a half a crop of corn, no way."

The little boy said, "No sir, that's all we working for—just a half crop."

"Son," the salesman said, "you know something? There's not much difference between you and a fool, are there?"

"No sir, nothing except a fence."

So that traveling salesman, he said, "Get up there, Maude!" And he hit the old horse with his switch and down the road they went.

Version B

This family lived close to the road in the country, and they were very poor people; they worked on halves. I guess the landlord, he furnished the land, and the tenant furnished the labor and helped with fertilizer, and they split the proceeds. At the end of the year, that is.

So a salesman came along the road driving a horse and buggy, and he saw the little boy plowing out there. The little boy was plowing right out to the rail fence that was between the salesman and the road. The salesman, he wadn't in no hurry; he just decided he would stop by and make conversation with the little boy.

The little boy, he was tired and he was hot, and the little ole corn did look mighty bad. It didn't have much fertilizer on it. So, the salesman started up and said, "Good morning, son."

The little boy said, "Good morning, sir."

Well, the salesman said, "Son your corn looks mighty yeller."

The little boy says, "Yes sir. We planted the yeller kind."

The salesman said, "Well, I don't believe you're going to make any more than a half a crop anyway."

Little boy said, "No sir. That's all we's working for—just a half a crop."

The salesman said, "Well, son, there's not much difference between you and a fool, are there?"

The little boy said, "No sir. Nothing except the fence."

In the first recording, much more detail and explanation are given. The salesman's horse is even named, a name used twice within the story. The explanatory information about sharecropping is given in simpler terms in the first account where there are children present. And even the language used in dialogue has more informality than in the second version. The greeting, for example, is "Howdy" rather than "Good morning." Stith Thompson asks the question, "How much liberty does the taleteller feel justified in taking with his stylistic effects?" The answer, he said, seems "to be that the skillful raconteur usually handles his material very freely, but within traditional limits. There are certain commonplaces of event or background or of work order so traditional that they are an indispensable part of the manner of the storyteller" (*The Folktale*, p. 450). Mr. Glenn does keep within the traditional limits, maintaining almost identical phraseology in the key punch lines in both stories.

Linda Dégh, while discussing the social function of storytelling, presents a very interesting discussion on the authenticity of the tale—what it is that makes the story believable. She suggests one fundamental rule for the folktale: "The storyteller is free to lie away to his heart's content but must not be caught in his lies. . . . Yet the storyteller does, of course, everything in his power to make his stories sound true." Consequently, he employs what Dégh calls "all sorts of artistic tricks" to make his audience believe that which they know to be lies (p. 133). Some of these devices include the introductory and concluding formulas, use of witnesses to substantiate a story, and a detailed description of the scene of the tale.

The study of opening and closing formulas, according to Russell Reaver of Florida State University, has been relatively neglected. In his 1972 article "From Reality to Fantasy: Opening-Closing Formulas in the Structure of American Tall Tales," he states that "narratives are patterned by various degrees of motivation to begin and end the tales." The openings prepare the audience for the adventure to come; the closings round off the events, "keeping the tonality of comedy or tragicomedy consistent."[7] Mr. Glenn and Mr. Womble both employ opening- and closing-formula phrases in some of their tales, especially the long ones. Mr. Glenn likes to set many of his tales back in time with such phrases as "This happened years ago in the old horse-and-buggy days," or "Years ago in the fall of the year," or "This one I liked a long time ago." One of Mr. Womble's stories also begins, "A long time ago in this part of the country, in south Georgia . . ." Closing formulas run the gamut from such common endings as "Well, now that was about the last of that tale" to a more imaginative one used by Mr. Glenn repeatedly (though in only one recorded here): "Of course I couldn't hang around, because I had on paper clothes, and I was afraid the wind might blow or it might rain" (tale 1).

Mr. Womble gave his witch tales credence and authority by attributing them to a real witch named Ila Gilly he supposedly met in Bancroft, Georgia. He said, "I do feel that maybe Ila Gilly really was a witch, for some very unusual things happened to us which were mighty peculiar." After the tales had been told, he brought them all to a close by relating a "true" happening while he was in Bancroft:

> On the last night we sat with Ila the strangest thing happened. We all wanted her to tell us some more stories, so she said, "All right, I've got the best one of all." Well, we were all set to hear a really good one. She began the story, but before we could tell whether it was the truth or a lie, every door in that house opened at the same time. . . . Can you imagine that every knob turned—and it was wintertime like I said—and then every door fell open! And old Ila almost went into spasms! She was scared to

---

7. Russell Reaver, "From Reality to Fantasy: Opening-Closing Formulas in the Structure of American Tall Tales," *Southern Folklore Quarterly* 36 (1972): 380.

death. We always believed she was about to tell something she wasn't supposed to tell. . . . But, anyway, that was the last of the witch tales. (Interview, August 17, 1972)

The detailed use of setting, especially a local or a rural one, is used frequently by these two Georgia narrators to establish greater authenticity and reality. Many examples occur: "They didn't have hotels and motels as they do now, and this traveling salesman was going through the country driving a horse and buggy and selling his goods" (tale 1). "A long time ago in this part of the country, in South Georgia, people would, in the fall of the year, get a covered wagon and . . . they would take off to the coast" (tale 2). "It was hot weather, so there was plenty of horseflies and yellow flies down around the creeks and branches" (tale 12). Frequently, allusions are made to farming or to crops raised in the area, and these also make for greater authenticity. In Mr. Womble's tale "Ghost of a Baby," there is much descriptive detail given about the shed where the mules were kept. "They drove up in the yard and unhitched the mules and went to put 'em in the little old log crib, a shed with a cow stall on one side and a mule stable on the other" (tale 2). In fact, there are two tales built strictly around the love of tobacco—chewing tobacco, in particular. In Robert Glenn's "Thief Reformed by Frogs," the protagonist is a farmer who, desiring a chew of tobacco so badly, steals a piece from the store. When he hears the pond frogs crying, "Plug-a-tobacco, plug-a-tobacco, plug-a-tobacco," he, guilt ridden, flings the tobacco into the pond, saying, "Here! The whole world's got to know that I stole a plug of tobacco" (tale 24). In another tale by Mr. Glenn, "Worms in the Mouth" (tale 40), it is a black who professes such great love for his "balca" that he carries fishing worms in his mouth rather than in his pocket, saying, "Humph! You think I'd have them nasty things in there on my balca?"

The practice of sharecropping, which has been prevalent in Grady County for many years, is brought into the tale "Nothing Except the Fence" by Robert Glenn. In the second version of the tale, Glenn relates how the landlord "furnished the land, and the tenant furnished the labor and helped with fertilizer, and they split the proceeds." Here the young boy who is plowing the corn meets a salesman who comes up to the rail fence for a chat. This is a juxtaposition of the wise and the foolish, with the farmboy appearing to be the latter until the punch line. When the salesman asks, "There's not much difference between you and a fool, are there?" the little boy answers, "No sir, nothing except the fence" (tale 47).

173

Aside from the artistic devices used to obtain greater reality in the tales, the folk (or oral) narrator, according to J. L. Fischer, works to evoke emotions in his audience "by acting out the appropriate emotions, as well as by describing certain events which stimulate emotional reaction" (p. 237). Although Fischer emphasizes the importance of the histrionic aspect, he regrets that so few studies have been done on this. Both Mr. Womble and Mr. Glenn have great mimetic abilities, reproducing sounds of animals, dialects, and other noises to evoke the desired emotional effects. Mr. Glenn especially is an artist in sound effects—reproducing the dialect of the Irishman and blacks, the sounds of frogs, and the breaking of a dish of butter smashing against the floor.

Both men evoke emotion through extensive use of dialogue and repetition. All of the tales included in this study invoke dialogue which comes alive as each narrator projects himself into the character who is speaking. If the speaker is some supernatural creature as in "Racing a Ghost," Mr. Glenn assumes a low, monotone voice as he says, "There ain't nobody here but me and you" (tale 1). The use of repetition plays a key role in this tale and many others found in Grady County. In Mr. Womble's tale "How to Become a Witch," the suspense of the tale hangs upon the repeated statement "I give all between the top of my head and the bottom of my feet to the devil" (tale 5). The use of black dialogue in a repetitive sense is seen in "Dividing the Souls" (tale 28) by Mr. Glenn where the phrase "You take this'n; I'll take that'n" becomes almost a rhythmic cadence as the little boys divide out the nuts in the cemetery. These repetitions seem almost to weave a spell which brings out varying emotional responses in the audience.

Many other artistic devices could be explored, for the whole story-telling event is a highly complex one, involving voice intonation, inflection, gestures, facial expressions, pauses, all involved with the very essence of the narrator himself. These, however, are harder to study logically and systematically. It seems that the excellent storyteller has some kind of innate ability which enables him to capture and hold his audience. Linda Dégh goes so far as to suggest that the art of storytelling may even be a calling that the true raconteur prepares for all his life by constant observation (p. 137). Thus Mrs. Womble's statement about her husband may have much truth for all great narrators: "Tale-telling must've been born in him."

Appendix 3 · Folktale Motifs and Types

Classification of Motifs

Motif		Tale
	E. The Dead	
E332.3.1	Ghost rides on horseback with rider	4
E371.4	Ghost of man returns to point out buried treasure	3
E402.1.1.3	Ghost cries and screams	2
E422.1.11.4	Revenant as skeleton	2
E425.3	Revenant as child	2
E545.12	Ghost directs man to hidden treasure	3
E545.19.2	Proper means of addressing ghosts	3
E581.2	Dead person rides horse	4
	G. Ogres	
G211.1.1.2	Witch as horse shod with horseshoes	6
G211.1.1.2 (a)	Witch rides man after transforming him with magic bridle	6
G211.1.6	Witch as hog	7
G224.13.2	Initiation: person kneels, puts one hand under feet, other on head	5
G241.2.1	Witch transforms man to horse and rides him	6

175

Classification of Motifs

Motif		Tale

H. Tests

H1416	Fear test: staying in frightful place	27
H1411	Fear test: staying in haunted house	3

J. The Wise and the Foolish

J1260	Repartee based on church or clergy	36
J1262	Repartee based on doctrinal discussions	36
J1485	Mistaken identity	10
J1495.1	Man runs from actual or supposed ghost	1
J1495.3*	Man attempts to stay in haunted house all night	1
J1649 (e)	Person asks native where road goes	47
J1760	Animal or person mistaken for something else	32
J1769.2*	Dead man thought to be alive	37
J1772.1	Pumpkin thought to be ass's egg	8
J1782.1.2*	Sheep in abandoned church thought to be ghosts	22
GA J1785.9	Gasoline mistaken for urine	35
J1791.3	Diving for cheese	9
J1811.1.1	The old maid answers owl's hoot	17
J1811.5* (d)	Incorrigible thief hears frogs say "De-liver-up," reforms	24
J1811.5* (e)	Man in woods is scared by frogs	23
J1813.8	Sheep's head has eaten dumplings	48
J1818.2*	Ass kicks at flies, gets foot caught in the stirrup	12
J1874.1	Rider takes the meal-sack on his shoulders to relieve the ass of his burden	11

Classification of Motifs

Motif		Tale
J2133.5	Men hang down in a chain	9
J2259*	Absurd lack of logic: miscellaneous	13, 15

K. Deceptions

Motif		Tale
K1682.1	Big 'Fraid and Little 'Fraid. Man decides to frighten another	26
K1984	Girls keep up appearance to deceive suitors	18, 19, 20
K1984.5	Blind fiancée betrays self	16

N. Chance and Fate

Motif		Tale
N384.2 (a)	Death in the graveyard; person's clothing is caught	27

T. Sex

Motif		Tale
T255.1	The obstinate wife, cutting with knife or scissors	49

W. Traits of Character

Motif		Tale
W111.5.10.1	Lazy man is being taken to poorhouse or to cemetery to be buried alive	39

X. Humor

Motif		Tale
X411	Parson put to flight during sermon	31
X424 (a)	The devil in the cemetery	28
X435.1	"What says David?" The boy, "Pay your old debt."	29

177

Appendix 3

Classification of Motifs

Motif		Tale
X435.6	"Let Gabriel blow his horn"—boy obliges	31
X459	Miscellaneous jokes about preachers	33, 34
GA X459.1.4	Ousted minister asks congregation to note mistletoe attached to coattail	33
GA X459.2 (c)	Boy hunts rabbit for preacher's dinner	30
GA X459.1.5	Preacher confuses scripture	34
GA X599.3	Jokes on nuns	35
X750	Jokes on old maids	17, 21
X828*	Drunk person falls in open grave with humorous results	25
GA X1124.3.2	Lie: accidental discharge of gun kills ten hens and a rooster	41
GA X1232* (b)	Monkey trained to kill raccoons with gun	42
X1269*	Lies about woodpeckers	43
GA X1269* (b)	Large woodpecker flies out of log which is uncovered while digging a well	43
X1291	Lies about bedbugs	38
X1291 (a)	Large bedbugs	38
X1654.3.1* (a)	Hard rain goes into bunghole of barrel faster than it runs out both ends	44
X1655.2	Deep mud	45
GA X1655.2* (e)	Mud-hole so deep that mule almost drowns	45
X1731	Lies about falling	46
GA X1739.2	Man swallows carbolic acid	46
X1740	Absurd disregard of natural laws	46

Sources: Stith Thompson, *Motif-Index of Folk Literature,* 6 vols., revised edition (Bloomington: Indiana University Press, 1955–58); Ernest W. Baughman, *Type and Motif-Index of the Folktales of England and North America,* Indiana University Folklore Series, no. 20 (Bloomington: Indiana University Press, 1966). For asterisked numbers, see Baughman.

Classification of Types

Appendix 3

Classification of Types

Type		Tale
	The Stupid Man	
1676A	Big 'Fraid and Little 'Fraid	26
1676B	Clothing Caught in Graveyard	27
	Jokes about Parsons and Religious Orders	
1725	Jokes about Parson	30, 33, 34
1791	The Sexton Carries the Parson	28
1833A	"What Says David?"	29
1833J	Preacher Says: "Let Gabriel Blow His Horn!"	31
GA 1838A	The Possum in the Church	32
	Anecdotes about Other Groups of People	
1870	Jokes on Various Religions and Sects	36
	Tales of Lying	
1920	Contests in Lying	38
GA 1920I	Skillful Coon-Monkey	42
1951	Is Wood Split?	39

Sources: Antti Aarne, *The Types of the Folktale,* translated and enlarged by Stith Thompson, Folklore Fellows Communication, no. 184 (Helsinki: 1961); Ernest W. Baughman, *Type and Motif-Index of the Folktales of England and North America,* Indiana University Folklore Series, no. 20 (Bloomington: Indiana University Press, 1966).

Bibliography

County History

Brunton, Yvonne. *Grady County, Georgia: Some of Its History, Folk Architecture, and Families*. Jackson, Miss.: Quality Printers, 1979.

"Cairo–Grady County Story." Bulletin published by the Cairo–Grady County Chamber of Commerce. 1977.

Cairo Messenger. Feb. 5 and Dec. 9, 1904; Jan. 11, Mar. 22, Dec. 6, 1907; Apr. 2, 1920; Apr. 27, 1955.

Census of Agriculture. *Statistical Abstract for Southwest Georgia*. Camilla, Georgia: Southwest Georgia Area Planning and Development Commission, 1978.

Coleman, Kenneth, et al. *A History of Georgia*. Athens: University of Georgia Press, 1977.

Connell, Wessie. "One Library's Role in Adult Education." *Adult Leadership* 21, no. 6 (1972): 197–99.

"Economic Development Profile." Camilla, Georgia: Southwest Georgia Area Planning and Development Commission, 1979.

Grady County Collection. Roddenbery Memorial Library, Cairo, Georgia.

Grady, Henry W. *The New South: Writings and Speeches of Henry W. Grady*. Savannah: Beehive Press, 1971.

Mayfield, Marjorie. *Calvary, Georgia, Heritage, 1828–1977*. Cairo: Cairo Messenger, 1977.

Rogers, William W. *Antebellum Thomas County, 1825–1861*. Tallahassee: Florida State University Press, 1963.

———. *Thomas County, 1865–1900*. Tallahassee: Florida State University Press, 1973.

Thomasville Times-Enterprise. August 1, 1970.

Williams, Barbara. "A History of the Cairo, Georgia, Public Library." Master's thesis, Florida State University, 1961.

Bibliography

Interviews

Barrett, Athelone. Interview with author. Grady County, March 21, 1976.

Gandy, Early. Interview with author. Grady County. July 25, 1976.

Glenn, Robert. Interview with author. Grady County, May 6, 1972; October 29, 1974.

Hall, Alton. Interview with author. Grady County, August 29, 1976.

Mann, Leroy. Interview with author. Cairo, August 15, 1972.

Maxwell, M. P. Interview with author. Cairo, August 13, 1972.

Pope, Perry. Interview with author. Cairo, January 28, 1980.

Prince, Allie Ben. Interview with author. Grady County, July 1972.

Sellers, Alto. Interview with author. Grady County, September 11, 1975.

Singletary, Irven. Interview with author. Cairo, July 1972.

Trulock, G. B. Interview with author. Whigham, June 17, 1976.

Wilcox, Elmer. Interview with author. Cairo, August 3, 1976.

Williams, Barbara. Interview with author. Cairo, January 28, 1980.

Womble, Allen. Interview with author. Grady County, August 17, 1972.

Folklore in General

Books

Abrahams, Roger. *Deep Down in the Jungle.* Chicago: Aldine Publishing Co., 1970.

Briggs, Katherine M. *A Dictionary of British Folktales.* Vol. 2. Bloomington: Indiana University Press, 1970.

Briggs, Katherine, and Ruth L. Tongue, eds. *Folktales of England.* Folktales of the World Series. Chicago: University of Chicago Press, 1968.

Brunvand, Jan Harold, ed. *The Study of American Folklore.* New York: W. W. Norton and Co., 1968.

Clouston, William A. *The Book of Noodles: Stories of Simpletons; or, Fools and Their Follies.* London: Elliot Stock, 1888.

Dorson, Richard M. *American Negro Folktales.* Greenwich, Conn.: Fawcett Publications, 1967.

Bibliography

_____. *Bloodstoppers and Bearwalkers.* Cambridge: Harvard University Press, 1972.

_____. *Folklore and Folklife: An Introduction.* Chicago: University of Chicago Press, 1973.

_____. *Folklore: Selected Essays.* Bloomington: Indiana University Press, 1972.

Dundes, Alan, ed. *The Study of Folklore.* Englewood Cliffs, New Jersey: Prentice Hall, 1965.

_____. "Ways of Studying Folklore." In *Our Living Traditions,* edited by Tristram P. Coffin. New York: Basic Books, 1968.

Embler, Weller. *Methapor and Meaning.* Deland, Florida: Everett Edwards, 1966.

An Evening with Punch. London: Bradbury Agnew and Co., 1900.

Halpert, Herbert. "Folktales and Legends from the New Jersey Pines: A Collection and a Study." Ph.D. diss., Indiana University, 1947.

Hazlitt, William C., ed. *Shakespeare's Jest-Books.* London: 1864.

Jansen, William H. "Classifying Performance in the Study of Verbal Folklore." In *Studies in Folklore,* edited by W. Edson Richmond, pp. 110–18. Bloomington: Indiana University Press.

Leach, Maria, ed. *Standard Dictionary of Folklore, Mythology, and Legend.* Vol. 2. New York: Funk and Wagnalls, 1949.

Masterson, James R. *Tall Tales of Arkansas.* Boston: Chapman and Grimes, 1942.

Olrik, Axel. "Epic Laws of Folk Narrative." In *The Study of Folklore.* See Dundes.

Paredes, Américo, ed. and trans. *Folktales of Mexico.* Folktales of the World Series. Chicago: University of Chicago Press, 1970.

Paredes, Américo, and Richard Bauman, eds. *Towards New Perspectives in Folklore.* Austin: University of Texas Press, 1972.

Randolph, Vance. *The Devil's Pretty Daughter.* New York: Columbia University Press, 1955.

Reaver, J. Russell, and George W. Boswell. *Fundamentals of Folk Literature.* Oosterhout, Netherlands: Anthropological Publications, 1962.

Ruskin, John. Introduction to *German Popular Stories,* edited by London: Chatto and Windus, 1892.

Sachs, Curt. *The History of Musical Instruments.* New York: W. W. Norton and Co., 1940.

Sampson, George. *The Concise Cambridge History of English Literature.* 3rd ed. Cambridge: University Press, 1970.

183

Bibliography

Shibles, Warren A. *Metaphor: An Annotated Bibliography and History.* Whitewater, Wisconsin: Language Press, 1971.

Thompson, Stith. *The Folktale.* New York: Dryden Press, 1946.

Toelken, Barre. "The Folklore of Academe." In *The Study of American Folklore.* See Brunvand.

Twain, Mark, et al. *Wit and Humor of the Age.* San Francisco: Law, Kind and Law, 1884.

Zall, P. M. *A Hundred Merry Tales and Other English Jestbooks of the Fifteenth and Sixteenth Centuries.* Lincoln: University of Nebraska Press, 1963.

Indexes

Aarne, Antti. *The Types of the Folktale.* Translated and enlarged by Stith Thompson. Folklore Fellows Communication, no. 184. Helsinki: 1961.

Baughman, Ernest W. *Type and Motif-Index of the Folktales of England and North America.* Indiana University Folklore Series, no. 20. Bloomington: Indiana University Press, 1966.

Thompson, Stith. *Motif-Index of Folk Literature.* 6 Vols. Revised Edition. Bloomington: Indiana University Press, 1955–58.

_____. *The Types of the Folktale.* Helsinki: Folklore Fellow Communication, no. 184, 1961.

Articles

Abrahams, Roger. "On Meaning and Gaming." JAF 82 (1969): 268–70.

Bascom, William. "The Forms of Folklore: Prose Narrative." JAF 78 (1965): 3–20.

Ben-Amos, Dan. "Toward a Definition of Folklore in Context." JAF 84 (1971): 3–15.

Boggs, Ralph Steel. "North Carolina White Folktales and Riddles." JAF 47 (1934): 289–328.

Brewster, Paul G. "Old Wine in New Bottles." *Hoosier Folklore Bulletin* 3 (1944): 19–20.

Brunvand, Jan Harold. "New Directions for the Study of American Folklore." *Folklore* 82 (1971): 25–35.

Cashion, Gerald. "Folklore, Kinesiological Folklore, and the Macro-

Bibliography

Folklore Complex." *Folklore Forum.* Bibliographic and Special Series, no. 12 (1974).

Dégh, Linda. "Some Questions of the Social Functions of Storytelling." *Acta Ethnographica* 6 (1957–58): 91–146.

Duncan, Emrich. " 'Folk-Lore': William John Thomas." *California Folklore Quarterly* 5 (1946): 355–74.

Fischer, J. L. "The Sociopsychological Analysis of Folktales." *Current Anthropology* 4 (1963): 235–94.

Paredes, Américo. *JAF* 84 (1971): iii–iv.

Reaver, J. Russell. "From Reality to Fantasy: Opening and Closing Formulas in the Structure of American Tall Tales." *Southern Folklore Quarterly* 36 (1972): 369–82.

Taylor, Archer. "The Problems of Folklore." *JAF* 59 (1946): 101–7.

Thompson, Stith. "Folklore at Midcentury." *Midwest Folklore* 1 (1951): 5–12.

_____. Myths and Folktales." *JAF* 68 (1955): 482–88.

Wilson, Gordon. "Mammoth Cave Words—More Neighborhood Doings." *Kentucky Folklore Record* 11 (1965): 52–55.

Index